GO TO
Yourself

Transformation through Jewish Wisdom and Psychology

MOSAICA PRESS

GO TO
Yourself

Transformation through Jewish Wisdom and Psychology

Aryeh Sampson

Mosaica Press, Inc.

© 2016 by Mosaica Press

Designed and typeset by Brocha Mirel Strizower

Published and distributed by:

Mosaica Press, Inc.

www.mosaicapress.com

info@mosaicapress.com

"God said to Abram — go for yourself, from your land, your birth place, and your father's house to the land I will show you."

Genesis 12:1

"Go for yourself," so that he would go to himself.

Malbim — Rabbi Meir Leibush's commentary on Genesis 12:1

*This book is dedicated
in memory of my parents*

Stanley and Rena Sampson

*whose lives exemplified
facing challenges with courage
and who inspired all who knew them.*

שמואל קמנצקי
Rabbi S. Kamenetsky

2018 Upland Way
Philadelphia, PA 19131

Home: 215-473-2798
Study: 215-473-1212

י"ח אייר, תשע"ו

I welcome the opportunity to endorse and commend R' Aryeh Sampson's work, Go to Yourself.

This book is an important contribution to the body of work that addresses the interaction of modern day psychology with Torah values. Adapting concepts from Rav Yisrael Salanter's work Ohr Yisrael, the author shows how Torah principles can be utilized to benefit us in our daily life, using appropriate psychological tools and techniques.

Addressing many areas of human emotion, he demonstrates how, empowered with this approach, we can become better, more elevated people. The reader comes away not only a changed person but an inspired one too.

In an age which is so focused on externals, but so much in need of inner development, Rabbi Sampson has produced an admirable Torah guide for our troubled times. Go to Yourself is informative, easy-to-read, and powerful.

With good wishes,

S. Kamenetsky

בס"ד

Dayan Y. Abraham
London Beth Din

יהונתן אברהם
דיין ומו"צ
בית דין צדק לונדון והמדינה

טו אייר התשע"ו
23/05/16

I am delighted to write these words of approbation and recommendation for my good friend Rabbi Aryeh Sampson's new book entitled "Go To Yourself".

I have known R' Aryeh and his family for the best part of a decade. R' Aryeh, a noted and successful psychotherapist, has worked for years in both the fields of kiruv and psychotherapy, dealing with a wide range of issues including anxiety, depression and relationship problems with both singles and couples. He has had the opportunity of applying modern and professional psychotherapy methodology in tandem with his own novel approach gleaned from the writings of the founder of the Mussar movement and giant of Jewish thought, Rabbi Yisroel Lipkin of Salant. The successful combination of the two approaches led R' Aryeh to further fine tune his methods and this in turn provided him with the determination to share the outcome with a broader audience, both lay and professional. The result is this book.

In today's complex and confusing world we are witnessing increasing psychological challenges and mental health issues which require professional assistance and support. The approach outlined in this book will provide a highly beneficial and constructive addition to the armoury of the mental health professional and layman alike. In layman's terms R' Aryeh lays out his approach and sets out the practical steps for its implementation. I am confident that it will be well received and much appreciated by all.

I wish you, R' Aryeh, every success in your endeavours in the future. May you continue to be 'Mezake ess Horabim' and assist and uplift others with your pioneering work.

Hatzlacha Rabba

(Dayan) Y Abraham
Kehillas Toras Chaim

2 Hillcrest Avenue - London - NW11 0EN
Tel 020 8343 6270 Email dayan.abraham@bethdin.org.uk

Contents

Acknowledgments

There are many people whose help has been invaluable in making this book become a reality. I would like to thank two dear friends: Larry Miller, a talented writer, who has patiently and wisely advised me on every step of the writing of this book, and Ian Ritchie, who has given me constant support and encouragement.

Much of the early inspiration for the importance of self-development has come from my teacher, Rabbi Noach Weinberg, *zt"l*, whose teachings and example have had a profound effect on every aspect of my life.

I am very grateful for all the help I received from my brother Rabbi Chaim Sampson, Rabbi Chananya Silverman, Rebbetzin Andrea Silverman, Rabbi Raphael Shore, my devoted cousin Merle Favis, Calvin Sandiford, David Rose, Anthony Sharot, Juliet Laudau-Pope, and my psychotherapy supervisor Anthony Stadlen.

I am also indebted to those who took the time to read my manuscript, Rav Shmuel Kamenetsky, *shlita*, Dayan Yonasan Abraham, Rabbi Dr Akiva Tatz, Professor Tal Ben-Shahar, and Professor Windy Dryden.

Many thanks to Rabbis Doron Kornbluth and Yaacov Haber, as well as the entire team at Mosaica Press. Rabbi Doron Kornbluth, my editor, has been outstanding; I could not have wished for a more insightful editor. I am also grateful to Martyn Niman and King Bee Animation for the illustrations.

Finally, thanks to my beloved wife, Rachel Rina, who has given me the greatest support in writing this book and spent many hours reviewing it. Without her belief, advice, and hard work it would never have been possible.

Introduction

Life is filled with challenges. How we deal with these challenges dramatically affects the quality of our lives. We can try to ignore, escape, or blame them on others; or we can face them head on.

In *Go to Yourself*, I share an approach for viewing challenges as a call to look within and express our authentic selves more deeply. It is a path of personal transformation, in which problems become opportunities to gain greater fulfillment. This approach is based on Jewish thought and on insights from modern psychotherapy, and it addresses many of the key challenges that modern life presents.

The book's title was inspired by the account of one of Abraham's tests. God told Abraham to "go for yourself from your land, from your birthplace, and from your father's house to the land which I will show you."[1] The expression used in the Hebrew text, "*lech lecha*," meaning "go for yourself," also means "go to yourself," as challenges are here to help us discover and express our true selves.[2]

This book is the product of experiences and study that have shaped my life. Knowing how I arrived at these concepts may help readers to understand them more deeply, and I therefore share here a few highlights of my personal journey.

I was brought up in a traditional Jewish family in North London, England, and received only a very basic and uninspiring Jewish education in my youth. After my Bar Mitzvah, I had little interest in anything to do with Judaism.

One thing that did interest me was psychology. This may well have been due to what my family referred to as "Dad's accident." When I was eight years old, my father suffered a serious heart attack and fell into a coma for several months. The doctors said that he had sustained brain damage, and when he came out of the coma we learned that he had suffered significant memory loss. He could only recall early memories from his youth and he had to relearn many skills. My father had been a dentist, but after the heart attack, he was unable to return to work. The responsibility for the family fell onto my mother; she looked after my father, worked, and raised my brother and me. This was a very difficult time for all of us and I believe it caused me to become a more thoughtful and introspective person. As I prepared to complete high school, I decided to study psychology at university.

I remember chatting with a friend at school about our university aspirations. As we were talking on the school grounds, an elderly man walked by. The gentleman seemed to have an aura of contentment and wisdom about him. At that moment I had an insight into why I was pursuing psychology. I realized that I wanted to gain insight into myself in order to achieve a greater sense of inner contentment and to acquire the ability to help others. This insight gave me an understanding into what was subconsciously driving me and this has continued throughout my life, as an unspoken mission statement: a quest for understanding in order to heal and be healed.

Before going to university, I took some time off to visit Israel. During a visit to the Western Wall, I felt extremely moved by a sense of spirituality which inspired me to take some classes in Jewish thought while in Israel.

Much to my surprise, I found Judaism presented in an intelligent and non-judgmental way. I began to discover that there was meaning to its practices and a depth of wisdom and psychological insight in Jewish thought, all of which was new to me. This started a learning process that gradually led me to becoming observant.

After my trip, I went on to study psychology at university. In the course of my studies, I was struck by the limitations of psychology alone to solve man's deeper conflicts. I saw this to be a consequence of the fact that so much of psychological suffering was rooted in a lack of meaning and spirituality. This insight was pivotal in my decision to change my career direction and to enter the field of Jewish education.

I then studied Judaism in Israel for a number of years and received rabbinical ordination. I returned to England and began work in informal Jewish education, where I taught and shared the beauty of Judaism with people who themselves had experienced limited Jewish education. Many of the classes which I enjoyed giving were based on the insights I had learned about achieving love, attaining happiness, and utilizing one's full potential.

I found this work very satisfying, but after close to ten years I began to feel that there was a part of me that was not being expressed — the psychotherapist within me. I started to dream about combining my love for Judaism with my passion for psychology.

I then began to study to be a psychotherapist. On the morning of my first lecture, I had been learning Talmud earlier and, not having had enough time to finish my learning, I put the book into my bag intending to complete it later that day. I entered the lecture room slightly late, and the lecturer had already begun with a talk on Sigmund Freud, the founder of modern psychotherapy. "Freud," the lecturer said, "was Jewish and his grandparents studied the Talmud." I looked down at my bag with the copy of the Talmud sticking out. It was as if I was being told that there is a special connection between Judaism and psychotherapy that I was about to discover.

I had many questions about Judaism's view of psychotherapy:

- Did Judaism believe in the concept of the subconscious?
- What is the root cause of our psychological issues?
- How can we best resolve these issues?

As I gave these questions more thought and studied a variety of approaches in psychotherapy, I began to gain clarity into these issues. I also saw how psychotherapy and Jewish thought could complement each other.

I was especially struck by a teaching of Rabbi Israel Salanter, who described three stages of personal transformation.[3] This concept became pivotal in helping me to integrate my understanding of Jewish thought and psychotherapy, and became the basis of this book. I call this three-stage process the ACTive method.

After establishing my own private psychotherapy practice and working in the field for many years, I have found the ACTive method to be profoundly helpful in assisting clients with a variety of issues.

My goal in writing this book is to share this method in the hope that it can enrich the lives of others. It is not meant as a replacement for psychotherapy, but is an additional tool for those seeking to grow and develop themselves. For a similar reason, I have developed workshops and seminars on this approach.

The book is written for both the layman and those with greater knowledge. I have therefore included an extensive glossary of psychological and Hebrew terms.

Part I of the book explains the theoretical basis of the ACTive method beginning with a description of the nature of the psyche and the roots of psychological problems. I then share Rabbi Salanter's three-stage approach for transformation and how Jewish thought and modern psychotherapy can assist in its application.

Part II explores the practical application of the ACTive method, applying it to three key areas of life: self, relationships, and spirituality.

The "Self" section addresses overcoming anxiety, defeating depression, and building self-esteem. The section titled "Relationships" deals with anger management, jealousy, love, and marriage. "Spirituality" deals with overcoming guilt, achieving moral integrity, and developing a deeper sense of meaning and spirituality.

Examples drawn from my psychotherapy work have been changed both in name and detail to maintain confidentiality. A set of questions follows many of the chapters to assist in the practical application of these concepts to our lives.

Part I
The ACTive Method

Chapter 1

The Psyche

*The area in which a person is deficient is the very area
in which lies one's potential for greatness.*

(Rabbi Tzadok HaCohen, *Tzidkat HaTzaddik* 70)

PSYCHOTHERAPY seeks to describe the source of psychological problems. Many explanations have been proposed which include a repression of instinctual drives, a traumatic upbringing, or a lack of meaning. In Jewish thought, the source is the understanding that man's nature has an internal duality.

When we look inside ourselves, we discover conflicts. Try completing a sentence beginning with the words, "I should..." or "I ought to..." and then ending with "but I... " You will probably finish by saying, "I'm too busy," or "it's too hard," or something to that effect. A part of us wants to do something and another part holds us back; these two sides of us are in conflict.

> For instance, we often experience an inner conflict when we feel angry with someone. One part of us wants to stay calm; an inner voice says, "Stay calm, don't lose your temper; it's not worth becoming upset," while another part of us says, "Give this person a piece of your mind, don't hold back!"

These conflicts are rooted in two aspects of the psyche: the true self and the deceptive self. The true self is our essence, which is good and has potential for greatness. The deceptive self is our darker, lower side — the part of us that opposes the true self. It creates tempting illusions that draw us away from that which we know to be true. In Hebrew, one of the many names for it is the "*sitra achra*," meaning the "other side."

When we tune in to our true selves, we find our inner sanity. In everyday language we call it our intuition, conscience, common sense, or inner wisdom. It guides us to do that which is truly in our best interest. The Talmud explains the innate source of this insight with the following cryptic idea.

> *When a baby is in its mother's womb, it is taught by an angel all the wisdom and moral values which it needs for life. Then, just before birth, an angel strikes the baby under the nose and the baby forgets everything that it has learned.*[4]

This teaching begs a question: what is the point of having learned all we need to know, only to forget? The answer is that although this knowledge is lost from our conscious mind, it remains in our subconscious, ready to be rediscovered.

When we have an insight or moment of clarity we often feel an inner resonance with the idea; it "rings true." This is because we are connecting with this inner wisdom. By listening to it, we are guided to a fulfilled life. As King Solomon advises, "Wisdom in the heart of man is like deep water, a man of understanding will draw it out."[5] I would suggest that while reading this book, a person is seeking those moments of clarity and will connect with this part of himself.

Listening to our deceptive selves, on the other hand, can be compared to listening to a young child who is only interested in gratifying his short-term wants and ego needs; it tries to convince us that it is in our best interest to follow its advice. For example, it may advise us to procrastinate and push off important activities, telling us we have plenty of time, or to eat whatever we set our eyes on, however unhealthy it is.

Listening to the deceptive side may provide a degree of instant gratification, but it ultimately leaves a person unfulfilled and dissatisfied. The more we listen to it, the more powerful and destructive it becomes, as the Talmud describes: "It starts off like a thin thread and over time becomes like a thick rope."[6]

The true self and the deceptive self vie for control of three powers: the faculties of thoughts, speech, and actions; with thought leading to speech and action.

The deceptive self is responsible for:
- Thoughts such as rationalizations, excuses, negative attitudes, and beliefs, critical self-talk, irrational, and illusory thinking.
- Speech in the form of inappropriate expressions of anger, slander, gossip, lies, shaming, and blaming.
- Actions which are self-defeating, impulsive, and reactive.

In contrast, the true self leads us to:
- Thoughts which bring intuitive clarity, wisdom, and common sense.
- Speech which is calm, considered, and appropriate.
- Actions which are productive, proactive, and responsible.

We may not be aware of many of these struggles, as much of them occur on a subconscious level. King Solomon describes the deceptive self using the term "the hidden one,"[7] as it hides within us, like the Dr. Jekyll within Mr. Hyde.

The Three Levels of the Psyche

These conflicts operate on three levels of our psyche:

1. The Intellectual/Spiritual level — in Hebrew, this is referred to as the *neshamah*,[8] and is the highest level of the psyche. It includes our intellect and our higher aspiration for morality, meaning, and a connection to God.
2. The Emotional level — in Hebrew, the *ruach*, which includes our feelings toward ourselves and others.
3. The Physical level — in Hebrew, the *nefesh*, which is the lowest aspect of the psyche, and the one we have in common with all living creatures. It is the life-force that guides the physical instincts of eating, sleeping, reproduction, and survival.

Our psychological issues are a product of these conflicts. Below are some examples of the problems that manifest themselves on different levels of the psyche.

Level of the psyche	True Self	Deceptive Self	Common problems
Intellectual/ Spiritual *Neshamah*	Pursuing morality, meaning, and spirituality	Following social pressures, seeking power, ignoring the spiritual realm	Midlife crisis, guilt, and depression (due to lack of meaning)
Emotional *Ruach*	Loving oneself and others	Hate, jealousy, anger, low self-worth	Relationship difficulties, divorce, low self-esteem, confidence issues
Physical *Nefesh*	Healthy physical pleasure	Excessive or unhealthy connection to physical pleasure	Alcohol, drug and gambling addictions, eating disorders, obesity

The unhappiness and destruction that one experiences are rooted in having lost touch with one's true self and its inner guide. We only have to read the news to see the damage this causes within society — with the dramatic growth of divorce, depression, anxiety, and a range of addictions.

The good news is that we can reconnect with our true selves at any time. When we hit a challenge or crisis in our life, we can use it as an opportunity to reconnect, to "go to yourself." Through these struggles we can transform our lives to achieve a greater sense of inner fulfillment and self-expression. In the following chapters we will examine how to achieve this.

Chapter 2

The ACTive Method
and Rabbi Israel Salanter

I created the deceptive self and I created the Torah as its cure.

(Talmud, *Bava Basra* 16a)

IN this chapter we will look at how to resolve psychological conflicts using the ACTive method. As I mentioned earlier, this method is based on Rabbi Salanter's three stages of transformation. We will begin by taking a brief look at Rabbi Salanter's life.

Rabbi Israel Salanter was born in Zagare, Lithuania, on November 3, 1810, the son of Rabbi Zev Wolf Lipkin, the rabbi of that town. He was a child prodigy and he became a tremendous scholar. After his marriage, he settled in Salant where he continued his studies. There, Rabbi Yosef Zundel of Salant had a great influence on him and encouraged him to study *mussar* — ethical teachings — on the topic of self-improvement.

In 1840, Rabbi Salanter left Salant, first taking a position as the head of a yeshiva, an academy of Jewish studies, in Vilna, and then going on to hold positions in France and Germany. While in these positions, he established his life mission — to revitalize European Jewry through teaching the importance of *mussar*, thus beginning the Mussar Movement.

He spread this movement by teaching the masses through public lectures, publishing *mussar* works, and developing an elite cadre of students who committed their lives to spreading the teachings of *mussar.*

There are many stories about Rabbi Salanter which illustrate his personal greatness and refined personality. One of my favorites tells of him walking to synagogue on the eve of Yom Kippur and hearing a baby crying hysterically. The baby's mother had gone to synagogue, leaving him with his six-year-old sister, who had fallen asleep. Even though the whole community was waiting for him to start the prayer service of Kol Nidre, Rabbi Salanter entered the house, fed the baby, and put him to sleep. As he was about to leave, the baby's sister woke up and begged him to stay as she was scared to be left alone in the house. He remained there and prayed the Kol Nidre service while holding the baby. When he eventually entered the synagogue later that evening he looked disheveled. Rabbi Salanter explained to the congregants with a smile what had happened, adding that the baby had had a good time playing with his beard.[9]

The influence of the Mussar Movement continued after Rabbi Salanter's death, in 1883, through the scholars who were influenced by him. They, in turn, had their own students, many of whom became leading rabbis in the twentieth century and continued to spread the teachings of the Mussar Movement.

The ACTive Method

Rabbi Salanter's approach for creating personal transformation is based on three concepts: Awareness, Control, and Transformation.

We begin with Awareness, known in Hebrew as *hergesh*,[10] which means to gain self-knowledge, insight into oneself.

Control, known as *kevishah*,[11] comes next. It occurs after we have gained greater self-awareness and we take conscious control over the influences of the deceptive self. However in this stage, the urge to follow those influences still remains and needs to be guarded and kept in check.

And finally, Transformation, known as *tikkun*,[12] occurs — when the deceptive self is transformed to follow the wishes of the true self without resistance, and these two forces become unified.

To understand the stages, we can compare the true self to a horse trainer and the deceptive self to a horse. In the Awareness stage, the trainer invests time and energy in understanding the horse's nature to learn the best way to train it. Next, in the Control stage, the trainer learns to control the horse against the horse's will. In the Transformation stage, the horse becomes trained so well that it willingly follows the trainer's requests. Together they form a strong unified team, harnessing the horse's physical power by following the trainer's instructions.

> *Let's look at how the three stages would apply to Dan, who has an uncontrollable temper and is always shouting at his children:*
>
> 1. *In the Awareness stage, he gains insight into his anger. He becomes aware of the things he's telling himself when he gets angry; for example, that if his children don't listen to him immediately he is a poor parent, or that they don't have any respect for him. Although these analyses are false, he reacts through this negative prism and this triggers his anger.*
> 2. *In the Control stage, he learns to control himself and to prevent himself from exploding with anger when he becomes irritated by his children. Nevertheless, he needs to be constantly vigilant to resist the urge to lose his temper.*
> 3. *In the Transformation stage, Dan changes his nature so that he is no longer tempted to become angry with his children and he remains calm in these situations.*

The ACTive method is so called because it is derived from the three stages — **A**wareness, **C**ontrol, **T**ransformation. Its practical application uses insights from Jewish thought and approaches from psychotherapy. We will first look at approaches within Jewish thought, and in Chapter 3, we will look at psychological insights.

The ACTive Method in Jewish Thought

Rabbi Salanter taught several practical approaches to achieve the three stages. These included introspection, studying ethical works (works of *mussar*), and impassioned chanting. In the generations that followed his death, the Mussar Movement developed other approaches that met the needs of the time. We will look at many of these approaches as well as a broad range of insights from Jewish thought.

STAGE 1: AWARENESS

Rabbi Salanter preceded the advent of modern psychotherapy by describing the strong influence of the subconscious on our attitudes and behaviors. He explained that its influence is more powerful than our conscious motivations and illustrated this with the following example.

> *A teacher has a student (whom he loves) and a son (with whom he is very disappointed). They both live in his house. From a rational point of view, the pupil is much closer to him than his son. Yet if a fire breaks out in the middle of the night, the teacher, upon drowsily coming to his senses, will rush to save his son before his student. "Why is this?" asked Rabbi Salanter.*
>
> *He explained that the teacher's love for his son springs from the subconscious, which is more deeply ingrained in him than the love for his student, which is*

based upon reason and intellect. Therefore, when he awakes groggy from his sleep, his subconscious motivations will be aroused and overcome his conscious ones, causing him to run to save his son first.[13]

As our subconscious forces have such a strong effect on our behavior, he goes on to explain, it is critical to understand them. Without gaining this awareness into our subconscious, we have an inescapable tendency to become trapped in a web of self-deception. As he puts it, "As long as the force of [a person's] soul remains concealed in its roots, as long as it is in hiding from human comprehension, it will continue to shoot its arrows at man's conduct."[14]

In other words, ignorance is *not* bliss. The less we understand the forces at work inside us — the inner workings of our heart — the more they will harm us. Rabbi Salanter advised people to seek advice from others and to set aside regular times for self-reflection to gain greater awareness.

> "As long as a force of [a person's] soul remains concealed in its roots, as long as it is in hiding from human comprehension, it will continue to shoot its arrows at man's conduct."

Rabbi Shlomo Wolbe, a leading teacher of *mussar* in the twentieth century, also emphasized the importance of reflecting on one's childhood to gain self-insight, as most of one's behaviors and traits develop in this period.[15]

However, the deceptive self has many ploys to prevent us from gaining this awareness. Rabbi Moses Chaim Luzzatto (an eighteenth-century author of many *mussar* and philosophical works) explained that just as physical darkness stops us from seeing obstacles and distorts what we see, our spiritual darkness distorts our thinking, making our failings seem nonexistent, or maybe even advantageous.[16]

One of the strategies of the deceptive self is to keep us so busy that there is no time for self-reflection. Another is that even when our shortcomings are pointed out to us directly, we may still deny them or blame them on others. Denial and blaming are an old phenomenon.

> *After Adam and Eve ate of the forbidden fruit, they hid from God. When God asked Adam, "Did you eat the forbidden fruit?" Adam answered by blaming Eve; Eve, in turn, blamed the snake.*[17]

There is an amusing story that illustrates this stage of gaining awareness:

> *A king discovered that all of the kingdom's wheat for the coming year would make everyone who ate it go crazy. The king asked his advisor what he thought he should do. His advisor replied that the king should store some grain from this year's produce to eat the next year. The king responded that it would be impossible to set aside sufficient decent grain for everyone, and that if they put away stock for themselves, they would be the only ones who would be sane, and everyone else would be crazy and would look at them as if they were the crazy ones. The king continued that there was no choice but to eat the wheat; but before eating it, they should each make a mark on their foreheads. Then when they looked at each other they would see the mark and be able to remind themselves that they were crazy.*[18]
> *This advice helped the king and his advisor to remain one step ahead of the others. Everyone else would be crazy and not realize it; the king and his advisor would at least know they were crazy.*

By gaining awareness, we acknowledge and understand that we, too, are also a little crazy, whereas before, we were oblivious to it.

Put another way, without this awareness, a person is akin to a sick person who has an illness but does not realize it. But if the person recognizes something is wrong and sees a doctor, the doctor will then be able to diagnose and treat it. So too, on the psychological level, gaining awareness is the first step in recognizing the issue and will ultimately lead to its cure.

STAGE 2: CONTROL

In this stage, we go beyond awareness. The goal is to gain control over the influence of the deceptive self. To do this, we can use the powers of thought, speech, and action, either individually or in combination with each other.

2(a): Thought

To control the deceptive self, we need to understand that it is not in our best interest to follow its advice. Through honest reflection, we can see through the rationalizations and recognize the negative consequences of doing so.

The Code of Jewish Law describes how, when we wake up, we are enticed by the deceptive self to oversleep. In the winter, it tells us, "It's too cold to get up, stay in bed a little longer," and in the summer, "How can you get up, you haven't had enough sleep." When we recognize these suggestions as rationalizations, we can overcome their influence by challenging their validity.[19]

> A story is told of Rabbi Israel Meir Kagan, better known as the Chofetz Chaim, a leading rabbi of the twentieth century. In his old age, he woke up one morning and his deceptive self told him, "You're an old man, you should stay in bed." He responded, "You're

even older than me and you're already up." With that,
the Chofetz Chaim jumped out of bed.

If we would give thought to the negative consequences of listening to the advice of the deceptive self (such as oversleeping, which can make us late for work and waste valuable time), we would be motivated to overcome it. As the Talmud teaches: "A wise person is one who sees the consequences of his actions."[20]

> "A wise person is one who sees the consequences of his actions."

> *My Aunt Diana was a chain smoker. During a visit to her doctor, she discussed giving up smoking. The doctor then did something unusual. He escorted her to a hospital ward to visit people suffering from lung cancer. Seeing the consequences of smoking so shocked her that she vowed, on the spot, to quit smoking.*
>
> *Gaining an understanding of the consequences of her actions (in such a graphic way) helped my aunt overcome her desire to smoke. She didn't touch another cigarette for the rest of her life.*

One of the reasons Rabbi Salanter emphasized learning ethical teachings, *mussar*, was for this purpose: It builds understanding of the consequences of following the deceptive self and strengthens the resolve to overcome it.[21]

2(b): Speech

Using our ability to communicate is another way to overcome and control the deceptive self. When we discuss something, we are forced to articulate our thoughts and feelings. We can then listen to ourselves and receive feedback from others, which helps us to see through the fallacies in our thinking and in our emotional state.

For this reason, King Solomon wrote, "If there is worry in a person's heart, articulate it, and a good word will turn it into joy."[22] Speaking about our worries helps us to clarify them. Receiving "a good word," benefiting from another person's input, can also give us a new perspective into our challenges.

The following story (even though it did not occur in a counseling setting) demonstrates the power of how a remark from another person can change one's entire perspective and help him see through rationalizations.

> *Two men visited the Ohr Somayach, Rabbi Meir Simcha of Dvinsk, with a dispute regarding the ownership of a piece of land. The rabbi listened to both sides but could not decide who was in the right. He tried to persuade both parties to reach a compromised agreement but each stubbornly refused. He then requested that they all go to view the piece of land.*
>
> *When they arrived, the rabbi put his ear to the land. The rabbi then said, "Each of you has good claims and both declare, "The land is mine." But the land declares, "You are both mine!" The two men understood the point that the rabbi was making, that they would both end up buried in the land one day.*
>
> *They then realized the pettiness of their argument and went on to resolve their dispute.[23]*

There is another important aspect of speech: It allows us to vent our negative feelings, thus reducing their impact. Once we are able to get something off our chests and unburden ourselves, we naturally feel better.[24] This reduces our desire to lash out and act in ways that would be harmful to ourselves and others.

2(c): Action

By changing our actions we can also overcome the deceptive self. This concept is based on the teaching that "our emotions and thoughts are drawn after our actions."[25] By changing our actions, we change our negative thinking, feelings, and behaviors. Let's look at a few examples.

Rabbi Yosef Y. Horwitz, known as the Alter of Novardok, was a student of Rabbi Salanter. He taught his own students to overcome the fear of being judged by others — peer pressure — by asking them to deliberately do something in public that would be embarrassing. For example, he would send students to ask for screws at a bakery, or for bread at a hardware store. Facing the fear of being embarrassed and "getting past it" taught them to overcome the fear of social disapproval by realizing that it was greatly out of proportion with reality.[26]

Rabbi Nachman of Breslov, a great Chassidic master, demonstrated the power of taking action with the following story:

> *Once, a prince became insane and thought he was a turkey. He crawled under the table, removed his clothes and began pecking at the food on the floor. The king was very distressed, but none of his physicians were able to cure the prince. Then a sage offered to cure him. The sage joined the prince under the table, removed his clothing and started acting like a turkey. The prince asked the sage what he was doing, to which he replied, "I am also a turkey."*
>
> *They soon became friends, and one day the sage put on a jacket. The prince asked him what he was doing. He explained that a turkey can wear a jacket, so the prince copied him and put on a jacket. Then the sage put on trousers and explained to the prince that a turkey can also wear trousers. The prince copied him. The sage then came out from under the table and the*

> *prince copied him again. In this way, step by step, the*
> *sage went on to cure the prince completely.*[27]
>
> *The sage understood the powerful effects our ac-*
> *tions can have and the prince's new behaviors gradu-*
> *ally helped him to overcome his insanity.*

The following personal experience brought this insight home
to me:

> *While I was studying in Israel, I went through a diffi-*
> *cult period and I was feeling somewhat down. A friend*
> *of mine noticed that I was unhappy and suggested that*
> *I meet his rabbi. I agreed and we headed toward the*
> *rabbi's small synagogue in the Meah Shearim district*
> *of Jerusalem. My friend explained the situation to his*
> *rabbi, who then signaled to his students to form a*
> *circle. He took my hand and we all danced and sang*
> *together for about half an hour. As we danced, I slowly*
> *felt my mood shifting and I began to smile. When I left*
> *the synagogue, I felt as if a load had been lifted off me.*
>
> *My unhappiness had dissipated without a word*
> *spoken, and without a careful analysis of the problem.*
> *This came about through simple actions.*

By taking the right actions, we can overcome and control our
own deceptive selves.

STAGE 3: TRANSFORMATION

The Transformation stage goes beyond simply holding back the
urges of the deceptive self to changing our nature so that the
deceptive self freely follows the true self.

Rabbi Salanter developed an innovative technique of chanting ethical teachings as a means of achieving transformation.

Unfortunately, this skill has largely been lost, and in this book we will therefore focus on another powerful approach to achieve transformation.

The Rambam, one of the greatest rabbis of the twelfth century, taught that changing our nature and creating positive character traits takes place through repeating certain acts to form new habits.[28] These habits then become automatic — second nature. As the maxim goes: "Sow a thought, reap an action; sow an action, reap a habit; sow a habit, reap a character; sow a character, and reap a destiny."

The repetition of positive actions re-educates the deceptive self and its subconscious urges, which results in the deceptive self following the wishes of the true self. On a kabbalistic level, transformation is described as "turning darkness into light, bitterness to sweetness,"[29] as there is an energy shift from the deceptive self to the true self which causes these two forces to work together.

> "Sow a thought, reap an action; sow an action, reap a habit; sow a habit, reap a character; sow a character, and reap a destiny."

Consider a greedy person with an aversion to giving to others. If he were to repeatedly give charity to other people, many times over, he would gradually accustom himself to lose his aversion to giving, until he ultimately would start to enjoy giving and become a generous person.

Similarly, if you want to start an exercise regime and have not exercised regularly before, it can be a battle. Your deceptive self may tell you "it's too hard," or "you're too busy right now." But if you ignore these rationalizations and get moving, the more you exercise, the more your resistance to it will be reduced, and you'll gradually reach a point where you develop a positive affinity for exercise.

Through the power of *positive habit formation* we go beyond just holding back negative traits such as anger, jealousy, and anxiety, and replace them with positive ones such as generosity, responsibility, and proactivity.

Many people look for shortcuts — methods that promise instant transformation — in this process. Unfortunately these approaches often prove far from transformational, as the following story from the Talmud illustrates:

> *Rabbi Yehoshua ben Chananiah said, "Once a child got the better of me. I was traveling and I met a child at a crossroads. I asked him, 'Which way to the city?' and he answered, 'This way is short and long, and this way is long and short.'*
>
> *"I took the 'short and long' way. I soon reached the city but found my approach obstructed by gardens and orchards. So I retraced my steps and said to the child, 'My son, didn't you tell me that this is the short way?' The child answered, 'Did I not tell you that it is also long?'"*[30]

The Transformation stage is the long way that, in truth, is the short way. How long it takes can vary depending on the person and the individual issue. It requires time, patience, and determination, and often has its ups and downs. As King Solomon said, "A great person falls seven times and gets up seven times."[31] But with perseverance, the rewards are very great.

The ACTive Method and Jewish Thought

Stage 1: AWARENESS
Gaining self-insight

Through self-reflection and advice

Stage 2: CONTROL
Gaining control over the influence of the deceptive self

A. THOUGHT
Challenging the advice of the deceptive self and considering the consequences of following its advice

B. SPEECH
Articulating thoughts and feelings to another person and receiving feedback

C. ACTION
Taking action to overcome self-defeating thoughts, feelings, and behaviors

Stage 3: TRANSFORMATION
Changing one's nature so that the deceptive self follows the true self freely

Creating new habits through repeating positive actions

Chapter 3

Integration of Psychotherapy with the ACTive Method

There is nothing new under the sun.

(Ecclesiastes 1:9)

NOW let us look at how insights and techniques from a range of approaches in psychotherapy can assist the application of the ACTive Method. Many of these approaches are built on the same psychological principles found within Jewish thought, described in the last chapter.

STAGE 1: AWARENESS

As with Rabbi Salanter's Awareness stage, most psychological approaches begin by attaining greater self-insight. As Brant Cortright, Professor of Psychology at the California Institute of Integral Studies, wrote, "All of modern psychotherapy may be seen to be an intuitive groping toward a deeper source of wisdom."[32]

> "All of modern psychotherapy may be seen to be an intuitive groping toward a deeper source of wisdom."

People often begin therapy feeling anxious, upset, and confused. Therapists generally start by helping them explore their thoughts, feelings, and behaviors to give them greater insight and understanding into themselves, thus providing clarity into their subconscious by making the subconscious conscious. Great emphasis on discovering these subconscious motivations occurs in psychoanalytic therapy. It is not unusual to discover that people are unknowingly trapped in a cycle of negative thinking and self-defeating behavior.

Becoming aware of how and why our attitudes have shaped us is tremendously powerful. We can then begin to take conscious control of them. It is little wonder that the deceptive self tries to block this insight.

Psychotherapy (like Jewish thought) takes note of this "resistance" to gaining insight. Here are a few examples (described using psychoanalytic terminology) of factors that prevent us from doing this:[33]

1. **Projection** — subconsciously ascribing our own problems, feelings, or issues onto someone else. For example, a client who cannot admit to feeling inadequate may project their faults onto their therapist, who is then said to speak unclearly, miss the point, and be generally inadequate.

2. **Turning against self** — the opposite of projection. Here, a person doesn't allow himself to feel adversely toward others; rather, he directs these feelings inward. For example, a secretary working on a joint project with her boss may condemn herself for her boss's mistakes, rather than ascribing the mistakes to her boss. She thereby gets an overinflated attitude of the negative role she is playing, which will prevent her from gaining clarity into her difficulties. (We will explore this more deeply in Chapter 10.)

3. **Avoidance** — refusing to do something in order to prevent facing a situation. For example, a client may start missing therapy sessions or even drop out of therapy altogether due to a fear of looking at himself honestly.

4. **Denial** — refusing to admit something. For example, a person may deny his or her own role in hurting others or in the breakdown of a marriage.
5. **Repression** — forgetting something that is unpleasant to think about. For example, a client may totally forget an unpleasant experience or fact about himself, or even forget to show up to therapy at all, in order to avoid the pain it causes.

In psychotherapy, as in Jewish thought, it is important to discover the source of our self-defeating behavior. It may be an innate character trait, one that developed through time, or even a combination of the two. Psychotherapy places great emphasis on those character traits that have developed through painful or traumatic experiences in childhood.

It teaches that when a child feels hurt, wounded, and vulnerable due to painful or traumatic experiences, he develops certain attitudes and beliefs about the world and himself. "You can't trust people," "life is unfair," or "I am inadequate" are examples of the beliefs that form a kind of subconscious script that guides the child in his future life. The child may also develop maladaptive coping behaviors to help stay safe and avoid these painful situations from reoccurring.

There are many different forms of coping behaviors. Here arc a few examples:

- Social withdrawal to avoid the pain of hurtful relationships;
- Addictive behaviors to escape from painful feelings;
- Seeking approval from other people to feel better about oneself by becoming a high achiever, a people pleaser, or a perfectionist;
- Developing aggressive and narcissistic behaviors to build oneself up by controlling and dominating others.

These coping strategies may give some help in the short term, but often in later life they become the source of problems.

> *Nathan was very shy and had difficulty socializing and in forming long-term relationships. In therapy, it became clear that at the time his parents divorced when he was five years old, he felt abandoned. To protect himself from this pain, he withdrew from social interactions. This may have helped him at the time, but in later life his unresolved fears of abandonment caused him to have great difficulty in building relationships.*

STAGE 2: CONTROL

The next step is to look at controlling the influence of deceptive self. Modern psychotherapy, like Jewish thought, uses the faculties of thought, speech, and action to achieve this, with different psychological approaches placing different emphases on the use of these three functions.

2(a): Thought

One approach that places focus on the power of thought is cognitive therapy. This is a thought-oriented approach, in which irrational thoughts are challenged and replaced by more appropriate rational thinking. It describes a wide range of irrational patterns of thought, such as:[34]

- All-or-nothing thinking, where we see things in extremes without appreciating the spectrum of possibilities;
- Catastrophizing, where we predict the very worst outcome;
- Selective attention, where we ignore certain information and focus on other aspects.

> *In therapy, it became clear that Nathan's fears of creating social bonds were based on his belief that relationships were very painful experiences, in which people experience rejection and abandonment. His*

perspective came from irrational thinking, as he ig-
nored the positive aspects of relationships and magni-
fied their negative aspects. Using cognitive therapy, he
began to challenge his thought patterns to develop a
more realistic attitude to these social interactions, and
this helped him to overcome his fear.

Cognitive therapy has developed a number of techniques that assist in challenging unhelpful thinking. These include thought diaries, the downward arrow technique, and cost-benefit analysis. In Part II, we will examine these techniques more closely.

2(b): Speech

Psychotherapy can be described as a "talking cure," in which people who are struggling with problems speak out their issues. This helps them to achieve intellectual clarity and emotional relief through forming a confidential relationship with a psychotherapist.

Carl Rogers, originator of "person-centered therapy," believed that the *quality* of this relationship is the key factor in determining the success of psychotherapy.[35] A good client-therapist relationship enables clients to feel safe enough to share their innermost thoughts and feelings, and to be receptive to important feedback.

Sharing feelings from present or past experiences can also have a cathartic effect, helping a person to accept difficult experiences and to gain a new perspective.

In Nathan's case, he felt safe enough to express for
the first time his feelings of sadness, inadequacy, and
anger about the abandonment he experienced when his
parents divorced. By expressing these pent-up feelings,
he was able to view the breakup from an adult perspec-
tive. Rather than seeing it as a rejection of himself, he
realized that it was a problem in his parent's relationh
ship and that he, in fact, was loved by both parents.

This new perspective helped him to feel more worthy of love and to overcome his fear of rejection.

Apart from the creation of a good relationship with a psycho-therapist, which helps a person express his painful feelings, there are other techniques which can be helpful, including role-playing and the use of imagery, as found in Gestalt Therapy. For instance, in the "empty chair technique," a person imagines someone from his present or past sitting in an empty chair. He then speaks out his issues as if he was speaking directly to the person, in order to express and work through his painful feelings.

2(c): Action

Most therapeutic approaches seek to help clients bring an end to their self-defeating behaviors by taking action. Behavioral ther-apy, in particular, focuses purely on action-oriented techniques to bring about this change.

One example of this type of therapy is known as "systematic desensitization," in which a person who has a fear or phobia is gradually exposed, in small steps, to the feared situation or ob-ject. For example, a person who has a fear of dogs is gradually exposed to them. He may start by looking at pictures of dogs, then move on to viewing dogs from a distance, and in stages, continue to get closer to them. This progresses until he is comfortable with close contact with dogs.

Another similar example is called "paradoxical intention," when a client is encouraged to undertake the things which he fears. This approach in popular psychology is often described as "feel the fear and do it anyway." Take the following case:

A person refused to leave his house because every time he did, he became very fearful about his health. He was admitted to the hospital where he was given a thorough checkup and it was confirmed that there was nothing wrong with him. It was then suggested to him that he should go out on the street and try to deliberately have a heart attack. He followed the suggestion, and for the first time, the client was able to walk outside and break through his fears. [36]

A further commonly used technique is implementing relaxation exercises, which are used to overcome anxiety. A person inhales slowly to the count of a number, such as four, and then exhales slowly to the same number, in a similar way. This relaxes the body and the mind, helping the person to feel calmer.

Nathan was encouraged to overcome his fears by facing them and to stop avoiding social events to which he had been invited. He was encouraged to take small steps forward by attending such events and initially only staying for half an hour. He was also taught relaxation techniques to help him become more at ease while at these events.

STAGE 3: TRANSFORMATION

Not all therapies go beyond controlling conflicts to bring about transformation. One that does is cognitive behavioral therapy which operates by creating new habits through repeating positive behaviors.

Consider someone who has obsessive compulsive disorder (OCD). This person may check repeatedly to be certain that his front door is locked. The client is encouraged to gradually reduce the number of times he returns to check, until he checks just once. The act of closing it once, and only once, needs then to be repeated many times in order to have a lasting effect and to replace the old habit with a new one. When this occurs, the new habit becomes second nature, and there is no longer a struggle to accomplish it.

In Nathan's case (above), he was encouraged to have many more social interactions. This was difficult for him at first, but slowly, it became less trying. Over time, this created a new habit where he no longer feared socializing and he started to enjoy it.

Interestingly, Albert Ellis, one of the originators of CBT (Cognitive Behavioral Therapy), was extremely shy in his youth. Over time, he trained himself to overcome his fear of rejection by striking up conversations with hundreds of strangers in the Bronx Botanical Garden.[37]

The power of creating positive habits has also been illustrated in the abundance and popularity of psychology self-help books which show people how developing specific habits can transform them into "highly effective people."

Integration of Psychotherapy with the ACTive Method

Stage 1: AWARENESS
Gaining self-insight

Becoming aware through therapy of conscious and subconscious thinking, emotions, and behavior and their root cause. (Skills from psychoanalytical therapy can assist in this stage)

Stage 2: CONTROL
Gaining control over the influence of the deceptive self

A. THOUGHT
Challenging irrational thinking by using techniques from cognitive therapy

B. SPEECH
Sharing one's issues with a confidential professional person. Also using Gestalt techniques (role playing and imagery)

C. ACTION
Taking action to overcome psychological issues using behavioral therapy techniques such as systematic desensitization and relaxation technique

Stage 3: TRANSFORMATION
Changing one's nature so that the deceptive self follows the true self freely

Creating new habits through repeating positive actions, as described in cognitive behavioral therapy

Below is a practical exercise consisting of a set of questions to help apply some of the concepts we have introduced to one's own life. The aim of this exercise is to help the reader track down some of the main issues they may be struggling with and to understand the conflict between their true self and their deceptive self. At the end of each of the following chapters is a set of questions which can be used to apply the main principle of the ACTive method to one's life.

Exercise

Conflict between the True Self and the Deceptive Self

I. Create a list of up to three challenges or problems you are presently experiencing. (Write them in the chart below.)

2. For each one, answer the following sentence: I should do X but I feel like doing Y. (Write your answer to X in the true-self box and Y in the deceptive-self box.)

3. Does this conflict exist on the physical, emotional, or spiritual level of the psyche? (Put the answer in the level-of-the-psyche box.)

Challenge/Problem	True Self X	Deceptive Self Y	Level of the psyche

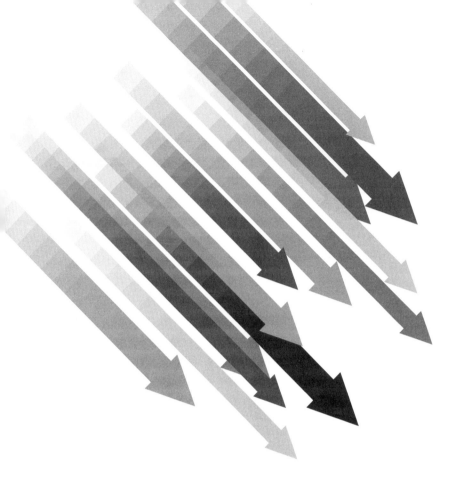

Part II
The ACTive Method in Practice

Section A:

Self

Chapter 4

Inner Calm — Overcoming Worry and Anxiety

*The whole world is a very narrow bridge
and the main thing is not to be afraid.*

(Rabbi Nachman of Breslov)

WE now begin the practical side of the book, applying the ACTive method to a range of psychological issues using insights from both Jewish thought and psychotherapy.

Our era has been described as the "age of anxiety," with modern man suffering from a wide range of anxiety disorders. These include general anxiety disorder, panic attacks, social anxiety, obsessive-compulsive disorder, post-traumatic stress disorder, and a range of phobias.

Let us look at the difference between worry and anxiety, and the relationship between the two. Worry occurs when we dwell on troublesome *thoughts*, whereas anxiety is the *emotion* which those thoughts produce. People often become trapped in a negative cycle as worried thoughts create anxious feelings which in turn cause negative behaviors. These behaviors then reinforce worrisome thoughts, as the diagram below illustrates.

57

Negative Thoughts:
Worried and
frightening
thoughts

Negative Behaviors:
Insomnia, eating less,
avoidance,
and procrastination

Negative Feelings:
Anxiety,
apprehension,
fear, and panic

STAGE 1: AWARENESS

The first step in overcoming worry and anxiety is to become aware of the nature and causes of our worrisome thoughts. This can be accomplished by using a method known as "the downward arrow technique"[38] (see Appendix 1). This simple approach starts with us recording our worries and then asking ourselves, "What would be the negative consequences if my worries were to come true?" Or, more simply put, "Why does this matter?" We record the answer to this question and then when addressing this new answer, we repeat the question, "Why does this matter?" We continue repeating this process until we reach the bottom line of our anxiety — the core fear or belief.

Josh, a computer programmer, worked for an IT company. His employer implemented some financial cutbacks and laid off a number of his colleagues. Josh then began to worry about losing his job and had trouble sleeping.

Applying the downward arrow technique to Josh's worries:

A. I am worried about losing my job.
   (Why does this matter?)

B. I will not be able to afford to keep up my mortgage payments on my house.
(Why does this matter?)

C. My house will be repossessed and I will become homeless.
(Why does this matter?)

D. Under this pressure, I am worried that my marriage will not survive and I will have a nervous breakdown.

This technique helps us to understand that although on the surface, Josh is worrying about losing his job, his bottom line fear — what is really scaring him — is that his marriage will collapse and he will have a nervous breakdown.

Sometimes our anxiety is rooted in difficult or traumatic experiences from the past in which we felt helpless, disempowered, or scared. For example, a child who was bitten by a dog may develop a fear of dogs, or someone who was trapped in an elevator for hours may develop claustrophobia.

> *In Josh's case, he grew up in a family where his parents struggled financially because his father was frequently out of work. This brought great strain on the family, and caused Josh to worry and to feel insecure. His father had a fierce temper and Josh was never able to express his feelings openly. As a result, Josh grew up to be very anxious about his financial situation, and this anxiety crippled his ability to be assertive in his financial matters.*

Josh's anxiety was caused by his early experiences and the lack of assertiveness that developed from them. There are many other traits that can contribute to being frequently in a state of anxiety, including an excessive need for control, procrastination, and perfectionism.

STAGE 2: CONTROL

Once we understand our worries and their source, we can start to control their negative influence. We do this using the powers of thought, speech, and action, either by focusing on one, two, or all three, in combination with each other.

2(a): Thought

Often anxiety is rooted in illusory thoughts. FEAR itself can be seen as an acronym for "False Evidence Appearing Real."

Illusionary thoughts can cause us to catastrophize — to blow issues out of proportion and to envision the worst possible scenario taking place. Memories of similar painful events from the past may also be projected onto the current situation, which further exacerbates the problem.

F — False
E — Evidence
A — Appearing
R — Real

I remember once waking up in the middle of the night with pain in my chest and upper neck. The pain was in the left side of my chest, and I began to think that I was having a heart attack. Thoughts of having a weak heart rushed through my mind, as my father had passed away due to a heart attack. I began to panic and sweat, having visions of being rushed to hospital by ambulance, surrounded by doctors and nurses. I started to think, "Is this it? Will I make it to the morning?" I woke up my wife, who called our doctor. After asking a few questions the doctor said, "This does not sound like a heart attack; have you been under a lot of stress recently?" I replied in the affirmative and he suggested I have a drink, try to sleep, and call him in the morning if I wasn't feeling better. I didn't need to call. Once I realized that there was nothing wrong with me physically, all my fears disappeared and I started to feel better. The tension in my body disappeared and I soon fell into a deep sleep.

Misinterpreting potential danger and visualizing the worst outcome are common causes of anxiety. People who have a fear of heights will tell themselves that they are in great danger of falling, even when they are in a perfectly safe high place. Those who have a fear of dogs see one three blocks away and immediately fear that it will attack them.

> *A tragic example of jumping to the worst conclusions is illustrated in the story of the spies who were sent by Moses to spy out the land of Canaan prior to its conquest. God performed a special miracle for the spies by ensuring that the local inhabitants were occupied with funerals so that the spies would not be observed. The spies also found very large fruit growing in the land, which they collected and took back with them. Instead of appreciating God's special protection and the goodness of the land that produced very large fruit, they became scared. On their return they reported that the Land of Israel is "a land that eats up its inhabitants" because they had witnessed so many funerals. The land is "a land where giants live," look at the enormous fruit it produces. As a result of their misinterpretations, the Jewish people also became scared and didn't believe that they would be able to conquer the land. This led to the Jewish people remaining in the desert for the next forty years.[39]*

To overcome the influence of self-deceptive thinking, cognitive therapy teaches that we need to challenge its validity. Asking ourselves some of the following questions can be very helpful:

1. Are there other plausible ways of seeing the situation that I am worrying about?
2. Is it possible that the thing(s) I am worrying about will not occur?

3. Even if the feared situation were to occur, will *all the negative consequences* that I anticipate inevitably come true?

4. Even if the worst consequences were to come true, how could I best cope with them?

> *I once had a client, Max, who was suffering from insomnia. He would worry the whole day about whether he would be able to fall asleep at night. I asked him, "What is the worst experience you have had with insomnia?"*
>
> *"I once went almost thirty-five hours without sleeping," he replied.*
>
> *"Then what happened?" I asked.*
>
> *"I fell asleep," Max said.*
>
> *I pointed out to him, "You did not have hallucinations, think you were going crazy, or become suicidal; you just fell asleep. The worst thing that is going to happen if you have difficulty falling asleep is that you feel drowsy for a long time and then you will fall asleep. If you can accept this level of unpleasantness you will worry a lot less about falling asleep."*

If we find after clarifying our worries that there are elements which are not illusory but real, we need to think about suitable solutions and create a proactive action plan to face these fears. We will look at this in greater depth in the section titled "Action."

2(b): Speech

King Solomon wrote, "If there is worry in the heart of a person, *yasichena* and a good word will turn it into joy."[40] The Talmud explains that *yasichena* has two possible meanings: to articulate the worry or to ignore it.[41] We will first focus on articulation and return to the second explanation later.

Articulation, expressing our thoughts and feelings, can help us gain a more productive perspective into the troubling issue, and reduce its negative emotional impact. As the idiom goes, "A trouble shared is a trouble halved."

> *One day, Josh met Daniel, his colleague and friend, for lunch. During the meal, Josh shared some of his worries.*
>
> *Josh: Since those people were laid off, I've been worrying about my own job. I've had difficulty sleeping at night and I've lost a lot of weight.*
>
> *Daniel: Don't you know how our boss always talks so highly about you and how invaluable you are to the company? They'd never fire you.*
>
> *Josh: So were the people who were laid off — at least that's what I thought. I keep on thinking if it happened to me, how would I survive? I won't be able to pay my mortgage and I could lose my house.*
>
> *Daniel: In the unlikely event of you losing your job, you could easily find another job in this field.*
>
> *Josh: It's not that easy in today's market — there are so many people looking for IT jobs, and a lot of them are far more knowledgeable about new IT developments than I am.*
>
> *Daniel: You can brush up on your skills. Anyway, you're always complaining about working for others. Why not start your own business? Hasn't that been your dream for a long time?*
>
> *Josh: Yes, but it scares me. What if I fail?*
>
> *Daniel: You could have a plan B — maybe working at your uncle's company. He's wanted you to work for him for years.*
>
> *Josh: I would have to accept a lower salary and the work is drab.*
>
> *Daniel: It sounds like you would rather worry about your situation than take some short-term practical steps.*
>
> *Josh: You may have a point there.*

Through this conversation, Josh gained some new insight. He realized that he had a number of different options he could take, and this helped him view his situation in a more positive light.

Josh also took his worries to therapy. He shared his present worries as well as his experiences as a child in which he never felt financially secure; something which he had always kept to himself. Expressing these fears helped him to feel less weighed down by them. He also realized that he was projecting fears from his early experiences onto the present one, which caused him to become more fearful than was necessary about the current situation.

2(c): Action

Taking action to overcome anxiety falls into two categories:

- Actions that help us to face our fears directly
- Actions that indirectly create a more positive sense of well-being

Facing the fear directly — When we have fears that are based in reality, we need to create a proactive plan to address them.

> When Jacob was returning to the Land of Israel after living with his uncle Lavan, Esau came to meet him with four hundred men. Jacob was terrified that Esau wanted to harm him and his family, as Esau blamed Jacob for taking his father Isaac's blessing from him. He prepared for the meeting with Esau by using a three-stage plan. He sent gifts to appease Esau, prepared for war, and prayed.[42]

Josh faced his fears directly by putting into action the following six-pronged plan.

1. He met with head hunters to assess his ability to find other jobs.
2. He started an evening course to brush up on his IT skills.
3. He looked into the possibility of starting his own business.
4. He arranged a meeting with his boss to discuss his long-term prospects with the company.
5. He spoke with his uncle about the option of working with him in the future.
6. He prayed for financial success.

As Josh started taking these actions, he felt less like the vulnerable child he had been in his youth and he became less worried.

Facing our worries head-on helps deal with the problem and calm our worries. One of the steps Josh took was to pray, which is also a powerful tool in lessening anxiety, and we will look at this in greater depth in Chapter 12.

Indirectly creating feelings of well-being — Getting back to King Solomon, the second explanation of *yasichena*, to ignore one's anxiety, can be achieved by focusing on other activities. This technique — distraction[43] — is also used successfully in cognitive behavioral therapy.

This seems, on the surface, to contradict almost everything we have said so far. True, completely ignoring our problems is risky and often leads to them getting worse. However, in some contexts, there are advantages to temporarily ignoring our anxiety. Activity creates distractions and interrupts the flow of frightening thoughts that cause the anxiety, and brings with it a feeling of calm. We can devote a certain amount of time to directly overcoming anxiety, and the rest of the time, we can ignore it through positive activity. Activities such as exercising, listening to music, walking in nature, and helping others can be very useful.

*I once ran a one-day education seminar for univer-
sity students in England. It was the first time this type
of seminar had been attempted. I booked a hall with
a capacity for about 150 people and worked on it day
and night for weeks. A few days before the program,
very few people had signed up for it. I was distraught.
I discussed the matter with my brother. He advised me,
saying, "You have done everything you can for this to
succeed, why don't you just take a day off and go for a
walk in Kenwood Park and chill?"*

*I took his advice and had a great day taking pho-
tos, reading, and enjoying the park's natural beauty. I
came back the next day feeling like a different person
and approached the seminar with a more relaxed attitude. Thank God, the seminar turned out to be a great
success — little did I know that these students did not
tend to book in advance!*

To summarize this stage — we can take control and reduce our
anxiety by challenging negative thinking, sharing our thoughts
and feelings with others, and by taking action to overcome the
issue and create a greater sense of well-being.

STAGE 3: TRANSFORMATION

In this third stage, we look at transforming ourselves by
changing the underlying character trait that causes the worry so
that we don't begin to worry in the first place.

*Josh's anxiety about his finances had, in the past,
paralyzed him from taking appropriate action and created a self-fulfilling prophecy. For him to transform his
anxiety he needed to develop greater assertiveness.
This became possible by repeatedly taking small steps*

to advance his financial situation. Initially this was very hard for him, but he slowly formed a new habit. He then began to face financial difficulties with a new sense of confidence, which helped him to view his future with optimism and calm.

When we repeat appropriate positive acts many times we gradually change these negative traits by creating new habits, and we uproot the root cause of our worry. For example, a person who is overly controlling needs to repeat actions that exhibit greater flexibility, and a procrastinator needs to repeat actions that are more proactive.

With these changes, a person becomes able to naturally move into a state of calmness and greater joy in life, as Rabbeinu Bachya, a twelfth-century rabbi from Spain, explained: "Joy dwells naturally in the heart when worry is removed."[44]

Exercise

Awareness

1. Think of a matter that is worrying you.
2. Use the downward arrow technique (see Appendix 1) to understand the bottom-line anxiety.
3. Identify if there is an underlying trait that is causing you to worry.

Control

THOUGHT

4. Is it possible that the thing you're worrying about will not occur?

5. Are there other plausible ways of seeing the situation?
6. Even if the feared situation were to occur, do all the negative consequences have to come true?
7. If the worst consequences were to come true, how could you best cope with it?

SPEECH

8. Share your worry with a supportive person and get feedback from them.
9. Pray for assistance.

ACTION

10. Write down a plan of action, breaking it down into manageable steps, and put it into action.
11. Do productive activities that create a greater sense of well-being in your life, for example, exercising or helping others.

Transformation

12. Repeat positive actions that will help you uproot the underlying trait causing your anxiety, until they become habitual.

Chapter 5

Happiness — Conquering Depression

Even if a sharp sword rests upon your neck do not give up hope.

(Talmud, *Berachos* 10a)

DEPRESSION is the number one psychological disorder affecting Western society, and its prevalence is growing at an alarming rate. Statistics show that a person born after 1945 is ten times more likely to become depressed than someone born before 1945.[45]

When people are depressed, they often experience a loss of energy, poor concentration, withdrawal from social activity, difficulty sleeping, and feelings of worthlessness. Fortunately, there are effective approaches to overcoming depression using the ACTive method, which we will explore in this section.

STAGE 1: AWARENESS

An important first step in overcoming depression is to become aware of one's negative thoughts, as depressed people are often caught up in a cycle of negative thinking. Cognitive therapy describes three elements of this thinking, known as the "depressive cognition triad."[46] These are negative thoughts about (1) oneself, (2) past and present experiences, and (3) the future.

Tania was thirty-four years old when her fiancée broke off their engagement. She was heartbroken and she became depressed. She started

1. *thinking of herself as a failure and unlovable,*
2. *dwelling on how unfair life seemed,*
3. *believing that she would never meet the right person in the future.*

It is also important to understand the source of depression, even though it can have many causes, including hereditary and biological factors. Depression is frequently triggered by difficult life events such as bereavement and redundancy, or a lack of fulfillment in life. A person might also discover that his own self-destructive behavior or counterproductive traits are playing a part in creating depression. Let's look at the following case.

Johnny became depressed when he lost his job. Initially he blamed his boss, but in therapy he discovered that the reason he was fired was rooted in his own behavior. He had grown up in a family where there was a lack of direction and boundaries provided by his parents. As a result, he lacked self-discipline and struggled academically at school. His lack of discipline followed him into later life as he could not dedicate himself to anything that demanded sustained effort. This resulted in his constant under-achievement at work and eventually led to his dismissal.

STAGE 2: CONTROL

In the control stage, we move from awareness of our negative thoughts and their cause to gaining control over depression.

2(a): Thought

Negative thinking in depression often occurs due to "selective attention," wherein people dwell on the negative aspects of a situation and ignore the positive side. One approach used in cognitive psychology to achieve a more balanced view is to record one's thoughts in a thought diary, and then to weigh the evidence for these thoughts as being true or false. This can assist a person in creating a new and more realistic perspective.

For example, let's consider Tania's case:

Situation	Negative Thoughts	Evidence Supporting Negative Thoughts	Evidence Against Negative Thoughts	Alternative Perspective
My fiancée broke off our engagement.	I will never get married. My life is hopeless.	I am thirty-four years old and I am not married. All my siblings were married earlier than me. Most of my friends are married.	Many people get married after the age of thirty-four. It is better to wait to marry the right person than to marry someone who isn't the right person for you.	I cannot predict the future but any number of people get married in their mid-thirties or later, so I can still be hopeful about my future.

Using the diary helped Tania to view her situation from a more positive perspective, rather than a hopeless one, and thus lifted her spirits.

There are many other ways to challenge negative thinking. One is to focus on *appreciating that which we do have*. There is an old Yiddish story that illustrates this approach.

> *Feivel was depressed about the cramped living conditions of his family of seven children. He went to his rabbi for advice on how to improve his situation. The rabbi said, "I have a solution. Bring a chicken into your house." The next day Feivel returned to the rabbi and said, "I did what you said, but it hasn't helped." The rabbi said, "Then bring a donkey into your house." Every day for a week, Feivel returned to his rabbi and told him that things were not improving. The rabbi then requested Feivel to bring another animal into his house. At the end of the week, Feivel exclaimed to his rabbi, "My situation hasn't improved, in fact it's gotten worse." The rabbi smiled and said, "Okay, now take all the animals out of your house." Feivel followed the rabbi's instruction, and then looked at his house and said to his wife happily, "Our rabbi is so wise! Look how much room we now have in our house!"*

Another way to deal with negative thoughts is to challenge one's thinking about the future. There is a legend regarding King Solomon that illustrates this approach.

> *King Solomon had a problem that sometimes he became so happy he would forget himself, and at other times, he would be very sad. One day, King Solomon challenged a jeweler who boasted that he was the greatest jeweler in the land. He said to him, "Make me*

a ring that if I am too happy I will look at it and become calm, and if I am too sad it will lift my spirits." King Solomon knew that no such ring existed. The jeweler replied, "How can any man create such a thing?" The jeweler then had an idea. The next day he rushed to the king with a ring. The king looked at it and said, "Indeed you have fulfilled my request." On the ring, it was written, "This too shall pass." Every time King Solomon looked at the ring he would reflect that both his happiness and sadness were only temporary states. This helped him to control his mood.

It is valuable to note that this is not just a helpful attitude, but that in reality the vast majority of cases of depression actually improve by themselves, without treatment, within three to six months.[47]

2(b): Speech

Depression has been described in psychotherapy as "a gift," as it can act as an opportunity for us to look more deeply at our life and to express ourselves in a more meaningful fashion. By sharing our troubles with a supportive person, we can overcome our depression by discovering the blind spots in our thinking and seeing beyond them.

Jack experienced depression and suicidal thoughts after his wife, Sonia, passed away. Jack had been married for over fifty years, and he had dedicated the last ten years of his life to caring for Sonia, who had been terminally ill. Without Sonia, Jack believed that there was no reason to carry on living. In therapy, his therapist asked him, "What would be the effect on your children and grandchildren if you committed suicide?"

"They'd all be devastated," he replied.

> *"What about your friends and neighbors?"*
>
> *"They would also be very upset."* Jack added that
> he had made many new friends in the hospital while
> he had been visiting his wife.
>
> *"Would they appreciate a visit from you?"* the ther-
> apist asked. Jack broke down in tears. *"They would."*
>
> *The therapist turned to him and said, "It seems that
> there are many people who value you and your contri-
> bution to their lives."*
>
> *The therapist's insights helped Jack to begin to view
> his life as having value without his beloved wife, and
> enabled him to gradually overcome his depression.*

Receiving emotional support through communication is also very important as depressed people often feel very alone and crave empathy. In Jewish thought, great emphasis is placed on giving support to people who are suffering from emotional upset as well as physical hardships. This includes visiting the sick, caring for widows and orphans, and comforting mourners. Ethics of the Fathers teaches, "Carry the burden of your friend"[48] — share his burdens and worries, because by doing this you will lighten his pain.

The traditional Jewish expression of condolence for a mourner is, "May God, *HaMakom,* comfort you amongst the mourners of Zion and Jerusalem." The statement is phrased in this way to remind mourners that they are not alone in their sorrow, but all of us are also mourners, as we mourn Zion and Jerusalem. The name of God used in this expression in Hebrew is *"HaMakom,"* which means "the Place," and is used to remind the mourner that there is no place where God is not; this is a subtle reminder to the mourner that he or she is never really alone, as God is everywhere.[49]

In therapy, showing empathy (which in turn helps the client to express their feelings) can play a dramatic role in helping overcome depression.

Esther was a young woman who lost her first child at the age of six months old. A few months after the shiva, she became depressed. In therapy, Esther reflected that at the time of the child's death, everyone had remarked on how well she had taken the loss. But this had been due to her putting on a strong front which prevented her from being able to mourn properly. Therapy allowed her an opportunity to express her true sadness, guilt, and anger. This brought her great relief and she regained her ability to rebuild her life in a more positive way.

Unfortunately, in more extreme cases, depressed people can sometimes go so far as attempting suicide, not because they want to end their lives, but as a call for help. A caring person who expresses a genuine interest, *even when there appears to be no immediate solution to another's troubles*, can have a dramatic impact on that person. This is evidenced by the numerous organizations around the world that are dedicated purely to providing a caring ear for those in desperate and suicidal states of mind.

2(c): Action

Taking action to resolve the underlying problem that is causing the depression is especially important.

In therapy, Tania explored the recurring cycle of hurtful and broken relationships in her life. She had grown up in an abusive family, and now realized that she had been drawn subconsciously to abusive and unreliable men, which was the source of her broken engagement.

She now started to make a conscious effort to meet men who were caring and responsible people. Although there was less instant familiarity, she soon was able to develop a relationship that was more stable, and ultimately more fulfilling.

When depression is rooted in a lack of meaning, taking steps to imbue life with a greater sense of purpose helps to overcome it. We will look at this in Section C ("Spirituality").

As well as taking direct steps to address the source of the depression, it is also important to keep active when feeling depressed. The Talmud explains, "Idleness is a cause of mental illness," as people with time on their hands often dwell on their problems, making themselves feel worse.[50] Or, put another way, Winston Churchill, who suffered from bouts of depression, is often quoted as saying: "If you're going through hell, keep going."[51]

Restoring activity levels, especially those that bring a sense of pleasure or achievement, is very valuable. Studies have shown that exercise, in particular, has an effect which is comparable to taking antidepressants.[52]

> "If you're going through hell, keep going."

Dr. Aaron Beck, one of the founders of cognitive behavioral therapy, recommended using a "Diary of Daily Activities,"[53] in which a person can plan the day ahead and fill it with productive activities.

Although counseling and psychotherapy may be very effective in dealing with depression, in certain cases, having the right medication can also be of value. In these cases, a doctor should be consulted to clarify whether this is advisable.

STAGE 3: TRANSFORMATION

The saddest day of the year in the Jewish calendar is Tisha B'Av, the ninth day of the month of Av. The goal of this fast day is to remember and learn from the destruction of the first and second Temples in Jerusalem and from other tragedies throughout Jewish history. Although it is an extremely sad day, it is also a source of motivation for self-improvement, in order to rectify problems from the past.

In a similar way, depression can lead us to new discoveries about ourselves and help us begin to understand the traits that cause depression and rectify them.

> *Through therapy, Jonny understood that his lack of discipline and his inability to sustain effort had caused him to lose his job and become depressed. He put his whole heart and soul into overcoming his past failings, and he started a new job working with underprivileged children. As Johnny began to help these children, he did several things that required sustained effort, and he started to develop a deeper sense of responsibility. He particularly enjoyed his work, as he was able to share and use his own personal experiences to help these children. Over a period of a few years, he gradually overcame his character flaws of laziness and irresponsibility, and he became a hard-working person. His new habits helped him to feel a greater sense of self-confidence in his ability to achieve the goals that he set for himself, and he developed a happier attitude toward life.*

The self-destructive traits that can lie at the root of depression, such as laziness, anger, or low self-esteem, can vary considerably from person to person. By repeating the appropriate positive actions that produce new habits, one can develop new character traits that can prevent the reoccurrence of depression and help a person lead a happier and more fulfilled life.

Exercise

Awareness

1. At a time of depression, write down negative thoughts about yourself — past, present, and future.
2. Ask yourself if there are any key events or life situations that may have triggered the depression.
3. Identify if there are any underlying traits that are at the root of the depression.

Control

THOUGHT
4. Use a thought diary to examine other more helpful ways of viewing your issue or situation. (A copy of the thought diary can be found in the appendices.)

SPEECH
5. Share your thoughts and feelings with a supportive person and gain feedback from him or her.

ACTION
6. Write down a plan of action to address the depression, breaking it down into manageable action steps.
7. Fill your life with productive and pleasurable activities.

Transformation

8. Repeat appropriate actions to form a new habit that changes the underlying trait that is causing the depression.

Chapter 6

Building Self-Esteem

God created man in His own image.

(Genesis 1:27)

BEING "created in the image of God" implies that every one of us has intrinsic worth. Based on this concept, the Talmud teaches that a person is so valuable that "if one saves a single life, it is considered as if one saved the entire world."[54]

Unfortunately, many people lack self-worth and do not feel this way about themselves. The Chazon Ish, a leading rabbi of the twentieth century, said, "Every period in history has a disease... in our times this is low self-esteem."[55]

Low self-esteem causes a greater tendency toward psychological problems such as anger, depression, and a lack of self-confidence.

> "Every period in history has a disease... in our times this is low self-esteem."

When Moses sent spies on a reconnaissance mission to the land of Canaan, they encountered giant-like people. The spies later reported back, saying, "We were like grasshoppers in our eyes and so we were in their eyes." One would expect the spies to have put it differently, saying, "We were small in their eyes and this made us feel like grasshoppers in our eyes."

> *This phrasing teaches us that our self-perception affects the way we believe that we will be perceived by others. As the spies experienced a sense of inadequacy about themselves, being "like grasshoppers in their own eyes," they presumed that others viewed them in the same way — "and so we were in their eyes."[56] They projected their low self-esteem, causing themselves to feel a lack of self-confidence.*

Developing and maintaining a healthy sense of self-esteem is a vital factor in overcoming these issues.

> *There is a story of a soldier imprisoned in a Siberian labor camp in the early twentieth century. The soldier would wake up in the middle of the night, put on a torn piece of clothing, walk around the barracks, and then go back to sleep. After a number of nights, a fellow inmate, Rabbi Yaacov Galinski, asked him the reason for his strange behavior. He replied, "I am a General in the Latvian army that is fighting the Russian regime. The clothing I put on is all that remains of my General's uniform. Every night I wear it to remind myself that I am a General, and as long as I remember my own importance, the Russians will be unable to break me."[57]*

In a similar way, if we maintain a healthy appreciation of our own self-worth, we will be able to resist the destructive influences of the deceptive self and its potential ability to lower our self-esteem.

STAGE 1: AWARENESS

The first step in developing greater self-esteem is to become aware of self-critical thoughts and their source. Self-critical thoughts may arise as a single statement, such as, "You are worthless/a failure/unlovable," or as a whole tirade of abuse.

People often learn to identify themselves with these self-critical thoughts when going through painful experiences in childhood or adolescence. The psychoanalyst John Bowlby, a pioneer of attachment theory, explained that the roots of many psychological issues, including low self-esteem, stem from a lack of strong bonding between a child and his primary caregiver.[58]

Low self-esteem can also result from negative experiences at school, such as academic failure, mockery from teachers, and as a consequence of bullying. A survey of school children found that on average, sixty-nine percent of boys and sixty percent of girls in junior school were happy within themselves. But by the time they reached senior school, only forty-six percent of boys and twenty-nine percent of girls claimed this satisfaction.[59]

Feeling bad about oneself is very painful, and as a consequence, people frequently develop coping behaviors in order to alleviate this pain. Rabbi Yonah, who lived during the thirteenth century in Spain explained, "A person who thinks of himself as 'great' is often trying to find relief from painful feelings of low self-worth."[60] This insight was made famous by the twentieth-century psychotherapist Alfred Adler, who explained that people create superiority complexes in order to compensate for their feelings of inferiority.[61]

> *One Yom Kippur, a chazzan, the leader of the prayer service, stepped up to pray in front of the synagogue and started singing, "I am nothing, I am nothing." A congregant who was moved by this act of piety walked from the back of the synagogue to stand by the chazzan, and repeated alongside him, in a low tone, "I am also nothing, I am also nothing." The chazzan turned to the congregant with a scornful look and said, "Who do you think you are to come up here and say you're nothing?"*

There are many different types of coping behaviors people use in an attempt to deal with low self-esteem:

- Perfectionists strive to feel good about themselves by avoiding failure.
- High achievers try to gain recognition from others.
- Loners isolate themselves from others to avoid the pain of rejection.
- Addicts numb their inner pain through addictions.

Although these coping behaviors may assist a person in the short term, they cannot solve the underlying problem of low self-esteem. They merely cover it up, thereby repressing painful feelings as opposed to dealing with them.

> *Daniel went to therapy to deal with his depression after he failed an important examination at university. He could not understand why he was depressed, as he was generally a fairly happy person. In therapy,*

*he recalled that in his early school years he was con-
sidered a "nerd" by his classmates and that he had
been bullied. To gain the respect of his classmates,
he worked hard and became academically successful. In high school, this strategy worked well, but at
university the competition for high grades became
fiercer, and it was much more difficult to achieve
high results. When he failed the exam, he once again
experienced the feelings of low self-esteem which he
had repressed for all those years, and this led him to
become depressed.*

STAGE 2: CONTROL

2(a): Thought

To build self-esteem we need to challenge the validity of our
self-critical thoughts. This is what Daniel wrote in his thought diary:

Situation	Negative Thoughts	Evidence Supporting Negative Thoughts	Evidence Against Negative Thoughts	Alternative Perspective
Failing an examination at university.	I am a failure and am worthless.	I failed my exam which shows that I lack the ability to achieve decent grades at university.	I'm only human and everyone experiences times of failure. I can learn from these mistakes and do better in the future.	Just because I failed this exam does not mean that I am a failure.

By using the thought diary, Daniel changed his attitude from
seeing himself as a failure to viewing his situation as a temporary
defeat, which in turn raised his self-esteem.

Self-critical thoughts frequently originate from internalized messages that we received in the past. For example, a girl who was told by her older sister that she was self-centered and ugly is likely to internalize these messages, as children generally assume that statements made about them by their elders and authority figures are true. Realizing that the source of these critical thoughts emerge from past experiences, as opposed to being a voice of truth, also helps us to discredit their validity.

2(b): Speech

It is possible to challenge our critical thoughts *intellectually* as described above, but still have difficulty shedding one's sense of low self-esteem because the impact of the *emotional* experience that created them was so powerful. In these cases, it may be helpful to share those experiences and the feelings associated with them with a supportive person.

When we experience a sense of shame or inadequacy, there is a tendency to want to hide it from others. But in reality, sharing these painful feelings helps to normalize them. In psychotherapy, great emphasis is placed on creating a trusting and empathetic relationship, which helps us to feel safe enough to relate our painful feelings.

> *In therapy, Daniel expressed the shame, sadness, and anger he had experienced at school. This brought relief to the pain that he was carrying, and it allowed him to view the situation in a new light. Rather than regarding himself as a victim, he began to see the bullies as sad, misguided individuals, and as a result, he was able to value himself more clearly and positively.*

The expression of these emotions has a healing effect and can help someone realize that he does not need to blame himself for what has happened to him. This also leads to greater acceptance and forgiveness of any other parties involved.

Another approach to this is to use the Gestalt role-play technique in which one visualizes painful situations that occurred in the past. For example, if we experienced bullying as a child, like Daniel, we imagine that we are now the bullied child. We then imagine the bullies in front of us and express the thoughts and feelings which were unsaid at the time. By reliving the experience in the present, the painful feelings can be expressed, and we become able to view the situation from a more mature and positive perspective.

2(c): Action

As we saw earlier, in the chapters about depression and anxiety, taking action can lift our mood. As Martin Seligman, the pioneer of Positive Psychology and former president of the American Psychological Association, wrote: "We feel elevated and inspired when the exercise of will culminates in virtuous action."[62]

Actions can either be those that stop self-defeating copying behaviors, or positive actions that express our true selves more fully. On a practical level, a person can ask himself the question, "What can I do that would help me feel better about myself?"

> "We feel elevated and inspired when the exercise of will culminates in virtuous action."

Dena had developed a tendency to always take care of the needs of others before her own, which served to conceal her low self-esteem. She would never refuse anyone that asked her for help, but she secretly resented many of these people for taking advantage of her good nature. Through therapy, she began to politely decline requests for assistance from those who were taking advantage of her and started taking greater care of her own needs. These actions helped her to raise her sense of self-worth.

In Positive Psychology, great emphasis is placed on understanding one's natural strengths and utilizing them in a positive way.

Martin Seligman describes having an epiphany when gardening with his five-year-old daughter. Seligman was struck by the realization that raising children was far more than just fixing the things that were wrong with them. It was about identifying and amplifying their strengths and virtues, and helping them find the niche where they could utilize these positive traits to the fullest. He criticizes psychology, from Freud onward, for having been focused on merely correcting flaws.[63]

Positive Psychology therefore asks its clients to take a survey to identify their strengths and think about how they can use them every day at work, in their relationships, and to enjoy a more fulfilled and meaningful life.

This process of helping people recognize their strengths and express them, as Seligman describes, is central to Jewish thought and is emphasized by Rav Wolbe, who taught the importance of understanding individuals' strengths.[64] It was undertaken by Jacob before his death when he gave his sons specific and personalized blessings, pointing out their greatness as well as their weaknesses.[65] Rav Wolbe emphasizes the importance of understanding our strengths before focusing on shortcomings.

By expressing our own individual strengths, we raise our self-esteem.

STAGE 3: TRANSFORMATION

Just as we have learned to identify ourselves with our weaknesses, we can relearn to do the same with our inner goodness through repetition of positive actions.

> *In therapy, Daniel realized that his desire for high achievement was a cover for his low self-esteem. He made a decision to start to do things which he liked*

and were not guided by a need for approval. For example, he decided to learn to play the flute, something he had always wanted to do but had feared that he wouldn't do well enough in the eyes of others. At first it was very hard for him to let go of his fear of disapproval, but the more he played, the less he found that he cared about the reactions of others. He gradually started to take pleasure in his own self, irrespective of the thoughts of others, and he gradually overcame his fear of rejection. Through developing this new habit, he began to appreciate himself for who he truly was.

Daniel replaced his unhealthy drive for high achievement with the more positive habit of expressing his natural talents without fear of rejection, which then led him to gain self-acceptance. For other people, overcoming other negative traits and/or bringing out their natural good traits through creating positive habits will help them to reidentify with their own inner goodness. This creates a greater appreciation of self and brings greater happiness to all areas of one's life.

In the next section, we will look at creating loving relationships. These relationships are built on the foundation of having a healthy sense of self-esteem. As Judaism teaches, "Love your neighbor as yourself,"[66] since we first need to appreciate ourselves before we are able to truly appreciate others.

Exercise

Awareness

1. What is your critical inner voice telling you about yourself?
2. Are you aware of the origins of these critical thoughts?

3. Do you have a way of behaving, or a persona, that helps you to avoid painful thoughts and feelings of low self-esteem?

4. Identify any underlying traits that are at the root of low self-esteem.

Control

THOUGHT

5. Clarify the truth of your self-critical thoughts by using the thought diary to weigh the evidence for and against them. (*There is a copy of the thought diary in the appendices.*)

SPEECH

6. Share the painful feelings of low self-esteem with a supportive person. (*In some cases this may require professional help.*)

ACTION

7. Write down a list of actions that when taken would lift your self-esteem. These can include expressing your natural talents and aspirations more fully and/or stopping self-defeating behaviors.

Transformation

8. Repeat positive actions that uproot traits which cause low self-esteem, in order to form a new habit.

Section B:

Relationships

Chapter 7

Overcoming Anger

One slow to anger is better than a strong man, and a master of his passions is better than a conqueror of a city.

(Proverbs 16:32)

IF you have ever exploded with anger and regretted it shortly afterward, or felt yourself simmering with resentment for days, you will know how destructive anger can be. Anger can wreak havoc on our relationships and turn our lives into nightmares. Medical research has also shown that anger is detrimental to our health: According to recent studies, the risk of a heart attack increases nearly five-fold and the risk of a stroke rises more than three-fold in the two hours following an angry outburst.[67]

Applying the ACTive method can have a dramatic impact on one's ability to manage and transform anger.

> The risk of a heart attack increases nearly five-fold and the risk of a stroke rises more than three-fold in the two hours following an angry outburst.

STAGE 1: AWARENESS

The first step in overcoming anger is to understand angry thoughts and their source. This should be done when in a calm state of mind; if a person has recently exploded with anger, he should take some time to cool off before contemplating the above.

Then we can ask ourselves, "What was I thinking about when I became angry?" Once we have identified these thoughts, we ask, "Which thoughts caused the greatest upset?" It is particularly important to identify these thoughts, as they are the triggers of the anger. In cognitive therapy, these triggers are known as "hot thoughts."

> *Take the case of Rachel and Adam, who have been married for five years. One evening Adam came home an hour late from work without calling Rachel to let her know. Rachel had prepared a special supper which was now cold. When Adam finally arrived home, Rachel was extremely upset. She took one look at Adam as he walked through the front door and began to scream, "You..."*
>
> *If Rachel were to analyze the thought process that led to her outburst, she might become aware of the following inner dialogue:*
>
> *"I have asked him five times to let me know if he is going to come back late. He never listens. He is so inconsiderate and self-centered. He even forgot our anniversary last year. Ever since we were married he has been this way. My parents never really liked him and would have been much happier if I had married someone else. I must be an idiot for putting up with this. He just doesn't care about me!"*
>
> *What upset Rachel most and played a key role in triggering her anger — the hot thought — was the idea that Adam didn't seem to care about her. This was particularly painful because it hit her sense of self-worth, as anger is often brought about through a real or imagined affront to one's self-esteem.*

The source of anger can also come from projection. At times, we may become angry with someone but feel unable to express it directly and then project it onto others. A man who is angry with his boss at work but is afraid to express it directly may instead flare up at home with his wife or children.

Projection also occurs when we transfer feelings from past relationships to current ones. A child who is repeatedly told by a parent that he is lazy and will amount to nothing may not react at the time. Later in life, however, when his wife implies that he is lazy, he may respond with an unwarranted level of anger. This is because the pain of his earlier experiences has been reawakened and it intensifies the pain of his wife's statement, much like a person who has a sunburn "overreacts" when slapped by a friend on the burned area.

Our angry thoughts and feelings can also be rooted in our own self-defeating traits. In the Purim story, for example, Mordechai refused to bow down to Haman. Even though Haman was in a position of extreme power, was very wealthy, and had everything going for him, he was overwhelmed with anger at Mordechai's simple act of defiance. His anger was rooted in his arrogant and hateful personality.[68]

Understanding the roots of anger can be illuminating, as it can provide a deeper insight into oneself. As the Talmud explains, "In three things a person's true personality is revealed: in his cup (when drinking), in spending money, and in anger."[69]

STAGE 2: CONTROL

Once one has understood what is causing the anger, the next step is to learn to control it and to prevent it from recurring.

Although in all the other chapters I share methods to gain control using thought, speech, or action (either individually or in combination with each other), with anger I suggest a person first use some action-oriented approaches. This means that when a person is feeling that he is about to explode with anger, methods such as removing oneself from the situation, taking a few deep breaths, or counting to ten can be very effective. After doing this, and avoiding an explosion, we can use the following methods to gain control to help us avoid losing our temper in the future.

2(a): Thought

When we become angry, we often think very irrationally and blow things out of proportion. The things we are telling ourselves, which are triggering our anger, may be exaggerated or completely incorrect. We need to learn to look at these anger-provoking thoughts more objectively.

One of the most effective ways to do this is for us to try to see the situation from the other person's perspective. As Hillel the Elder, the spiritual leader of the Jewish People in the first century BCE, taught, "Do not judge your friend until you have stood in his place."[70] In other words, we are instructed to strive to see a situation from the other person's viewpoint by understanding his attitudes, motivation, and background. When a matter can be construed in either a negative or positive light, Jewish thought teaches us to "give the benefit of the doubt."[71]

> *Children can be very disobedient, especially when it comes to going to bed. I once told one of my children to "stay in your room and go to sleep!" for the tenth time, and then added, "Otherwise you are going to get a serious punishment." Immediately after saying this, my daughter walked out of her room. I was ready to lose it, but I stopped myself for a second to try to understand what was happening. "What are you doing?" I asked. "I just wanted to give you the goodnight kiss that I promised you," she said. I realized that I had totally misjudged what she was doing and instead of getting more upset, I gave her a big kiss and she went happily off to sleep.*

Cognitive therapy, as we saw earlier, uses "thought diaries" to help people look at situations more objectively and thus gain a better perspective. In this example, we will focus on gaining perspective on the most upsetting thought, the one that triggers the anger — the hot thought — rather than all of the thoughts associated with it.

This is done by recording in the diary all angry thoughts and underlining the most upsetting one. Next, the evidence for this hot thought being true and the evidence for it being false are evaluated in order to gain a more realistic and less hostile view. Apply this to Rachel's case:

Thought Diary

Situation	Negative Thoughts (underline the hot thought)	Evidence Supporting the Hot Thought	Evidence Against the Hot Thought	Alternative Perspective
Adam came home late from work without calling to let me know.	I have asked him five times to let me know if he is going to be coming home late. He is inconsiderate and self-centered. He forgot our anniversary last year. He has been this way since we got married. I must be an idiot for putting up with this. <u>He just doesn't care about me.</u>	He doesn't call or text to let me know when he'll be late. He forgot our anniversary. He does not seem to be listening to me when I talk.	He apologizes when he makes mistakes. He explained that he's under a lot of pressure at work which makes him a bit absent-minded. He enjoys spending time together. He says he loves me.	Adam is currently under a lot of pressure from work, which makes him very thoughtless at times, but he does care about me.

Using the thought diary helped Rachel reevaluate her opinion that Adam was uncaring, and to understand that he really does care, but that at times he can be quite self-involved and oblivious to her needs. This change of attitude helped her to be more understanding of Adam's thoughtless behavior and to become less angry about it.

Reflecting on how we may be projecting anger onto a situation also helps us to reduce it. This is because we acknowledge that the hurt we are experiencing is not all due to the person who presently appears to have wronged us, but has its origin in unresolved issues from other relationships or from within ourselves.

> As a child, Rachel had always felt overshadowed by her successful older sister, who was the apple of her parents' eyes. As a result, she grew up feeling unappreciated. When she felt unappreciated by Adam, it was even more painful, as it stirred up her angry feelings from the past, which she then projected onto Adam. Realizing this helped lessen her anger, as she understood that her upset was not just due to his behavior but due to her own oversensitivity in this area.

The process of forgiveness is another powerful way to release poisonous feelings of anger from being triggered. We will look at this in Chapter 10 when we deal with guilt and moral integrity.

2(b): Speech

Good communication is another important tool used to control anger. By expressing pent-up frustrations and building understanding, we begin to reduce anger and resolve difficult issues. Unfortunately, when we are angry, we often enter into either fight (external explosion) or flight (escape) mode. Judaism teaches the importance of expressing feelings of resentment directly, in a non-confrontational manner — "Do not hate your friend in your heart; you shall give *tochachah*, constructive criticism, to your neighbor."[72]

Matt lost his temper and physically attacked someone. His inability to control his temper also threatened to harm a number of his other relationships. In therapy, he recalled that he had been a very sensitive child, and had learned from a young age to become aggressive in order to protect his feelings from being hurt. This may have helped him when he was young, but this tendency followed him into adult life, and whenever he felt threatened, he would automatically become aggressive and abusive. He gradually learned how to express his angry feelings in a more open, non-confrontational way, which helped him to alleviate his aggressive and violent tendencies.

Communicating effectively takes skill and sensitivity. If this approach appeals to you, you may want to look at the speech section in Chapter 9, in which crucial aspects of how to effectively express oneself to resolve conflicts are explained.

There are times when the release of emotional hurt alone is enough to alleviate anger without requiring a direct conversation with other parties. This can be achieved by sharing angry feelings with an empathetic and confidential third party; for those more comfortable with written communication, you can express your feelings in a letter, written to the person with whom you are angry, but without sending the letter.

The Rebbe of Piaseczna recommended the practice of writing a letter and then reading it aloud in a private place. A person should then read it daily for two more days. He explained that this is effective because by expressing these negative feelings, a person's anger dissipates.[73]

This method was used successfully by Abraham Lincoln.[74] When he felt angry with someone, he would compose what he called a "hot letter." He would pile all of his anger into a letter, but he would never sign or send it; he would put the letter aside until his emotions cooled down.

There is a further step that I have personally found to be very helpful. Once you have written the letter and left it for a while, write an imagined reply from the person who it is written to and then write your response to that letter. This adds the dimension of understanding the viewpoint of the other person, with your response to it, which can further help to calm your anger.

2(c): Action

Sometimes, asking a person who is making you angry to act in a different way can be very effective.

In the case of Rachel and Adam, Rachel realized Adam had a tendency to be thoughtless about telling her when he would arrive home. To prevent herself from becoming angry, Rachel asked Adam if he would call her daily during his lunch break and let her know if he would be home on time.

However, there are also situations when waiting for others to change their actions (even if they are willing to do so) demands a lot of patience and can be very frustrating. It may be more effective for the person himself to take action to change the situation.

Imagine you are traveling through Europe with a friend. Your friend turns up thirty minutes late for everything, causing you to be late numerous times and to almost miss connecting flights. You could either become very angry with your friend for being so irresponsible, or take action to change the situation by planning the day's schedule more carefully and setting out thirty minutes early to avoid frustration.

There is, in addition, a tendency to blame others for making us angry and to ignore our own role in creating anger. When we are tired, hungry, and under stress, we are more prone to anger. By taking more responsibility in these areas we can reduce the likelihood of becoming angry. Here are a few examples of what we can do.

- Get enough sleep
- Eat properly
- Be more organized
- Use relaxation and breathing exercises

On a deeper level, we may need to take responsibility for the underlying insecurities or self-defeating character traits which play a role in creating anger. We will look deeper into this in the next stage, Transformation.

STAGE 3: TRANSFORMATION

Transformation brings us to a different level; it goes beyond simply controlling one's anger to being able to remain calm in the face of anger-provoking situations.

To illustrate this level, there is a story in the Talmud about Hillel the Elder, who was known for his great patience.

> *A person made a bet that he could make Hillel angry. The man arrived at Hillel's house on Friday afternoon, when Hillel was washing his hair in preparation for the Sabbath. He knocked on Hillel's door to ask him an irrelevant question. Hillel came out to answer the question and after answering it, he returned to wash his hair. He then knocked again with another irrelevant question. Hillel came out and answered him patiently and returned to washing himself. The man did this several more times and spoke to Hillel in a disrespectful manner. Each time, Hillel came out, answered him patiently and then returned to his Sabbath preparations.*
>
> *When he saw that he was not making Hillel angry, the man insulted Hillel saying, "If you are Hillel, the leader of Israel, there should be no more like you." Hillel replied, "Why, my son?" The man said, "Because you have caused me to lose 400 zuz." Hillel responded, "It is better for you to lose twice that amount than I should become angry with you."[75]*

Hillel's ability to stay calm lay in his humility. As a result, he did not become personally offended and was able to remain calm. This ability to stay calm develops as a result of continuously working on one's character traits, such as low self-esteem, a tendency to be over-controlling, and arrogance.

For example, the anger of a mother who reacts to her children not listening to her by losing her temper may be triggered by feelings that she is an inadequate parent. It upsets her because she realizes that there is a certain amount of truth in the things she was telling herself about the situation. For example, she may be too soft with her children and lack a firm approach. In this case, she needs to bring out in her personality a greater sense of strength and firmness. This needs to be practiced many, many times until it becomes a habit, her second nature. Then she will remain calm when her children refuse to listen to her, as the thought that she is an inadequate parent will no longer cause her to become angry because she will know it is simply not true.

In the case of Rachel and Adam, Rachel's lack of self-esteem caused her to be oversensitive and to anger easily. She overcame this by creating positive habits that helped her to express herself more fully (see Chapter 6). This led her to appreciate herself independently of how others viewed her. She was subsequently able to handle Adam's thoughtlessness without becoming upset, as she realized that Adam's behavior was a result of his own issues — not a reflection of a deficiency in her.

As with changing any character trait, it takes positive repetition to form new habits, and this requires time and patience, especially when dealing with a weakness in one's personality. But with perseverance, a person can train himself to remain calm and at peace with situations that would have previously infuriated him.

Exercise

Awareness

I. Think of a situation that made you angry (ideally one that could reoccur). Use the first column in the thought diary (appendix 1, chart 2b) to record your negative thoughts about the situation. Underline the most upsetting thought (the hot thought).

2. Ask yourself if you're projecting anger onto the present situation from negative feelings about yourself or any other relationship past or present?
3. Identify if there is an underlying insecurity, habit or trait that is at the root of the anger.

Control

THOUGHT

4. Using the next two columns of the thought diary, write the evidence that supports the hot thought and the evidence against it.
5. Evaluate the truth of the hot thought and think of a less hostile way of looking at the situation (fill in the last column).
6. Think about the situation from the point of view of the person you are upset with.

SPEECH

7. Write a letter to the person involved, expressing your upset, without sending it.
8. Where appropriate, have an open, non-judgmental chat with the person you're angry with, using the communication skills from Chapter 9.

ACTION

9. Take more responsibility by performing actions that reduce the chances of becoming angry again.

Transformation

10. Repeat positive actions that will help you uproot the trait that is at the root of your anger; do this until you are able to feel a sense of calm when these anger-provoking situations recur.

Chapter 8

Eliminating Jealousy

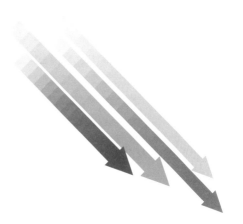

Jealousy... takes a person out of the world.

(Ethics of the Fathers 4:28)

WE live in a world where externalities, whether it be wealth, status, beauty, or other outward forms of success are greatly valued. As few people can "have it all," many people are left feeling lacking — which breeds jealousy. Jealousy not only robs us of happiness but can be very destructive. One just needs to listen to the news to see how it wreaks havoc and leads to hatred, cut-throat business competition, and crimes of passion. There are numerous biblical stories that recount the tragic consequences of jealousy, including Cain's murder of his brother Abel, the sale of Joseph by his brothers, and Korach's rebellion against Moses. In this chapter, we'll examine how the ACTive method can help us control and transform this powerful emotion.

STAGE 1: AWARENESS

The first stage requires us to become aware of the situations that arouse our jealousy and the thoughts associated with them.

Try, for example, to complete these sentences:

- I feel jealous when I see_____.
- What I tell myself when this happens is_____.
- It makes me feel_____about myself and_____ about my life.

Once we have become aware of these thoughts, we need to understand what is causing them. The triggers of jealousy can range dramatically from person to person, but it frequently occurs when we consciously (or subconsciously) are lacking something. For example, it is common to feel jealous when suffering from personal hardships, such as a financial crisis or sickness, when others appear to be blessed by better fortune.

Here are some other triggers:

When Cain and Abel brought sacrifices to God, Abel brought an offering from the best of his cattle, while

> *Cain brought an offering of vegetables. Abel's offering was accepted, while Cain's wasn't, and he became very jealous of Abel. God then asked Cain, "Why are you so angry? Why are you depressed? If you do well, won't your sacrifice be accepted?"[76]*

This communication was a call to Cain to introspect and to understand that the source of his upset was rooted in his own failure to bring an acceptable offering, and was not a consequence of his brother's success. Looking a little deeper, the name Cain is derived from the Hebrew word *koneh*, which means to acquire. His name described his essence; he was a person who liked to acquire and, as a result, found it difficult to give. His inability to bring a fitting offering and his jealousy of his brother were products of his failure to overcome his selfish nature.[77] A person's tendency to be jealous may likewise arise from an unwillingness to accept responsibility. The person then becomes jealous of those who have made adequate efforts to succeed.

Jealousy can also arise from a lack of self-esteem and confidence.

> *Ben became insanely jealous whenever he saw his wife in any form of conversation with other men, whether they were cousins, neighbors, or even shop assistants. His wife believed he was being controlling and that he wanted to keep her isolated from the world. In therapy, Ben realized that his jealousy was a product of his insecurities about his relationship with his wife. Ben lacked confidence and believed that he was unworthy of his wife's love. As a child, he had experienced rejection from some of his closest friends, and this had left him with a fear of rejection. Even though in later life his popularity grew, this fear remained and triggered his jealousy.*

STAGE 2: CONTROL

After we have clarified our jealous thoughts and their source, we move to the next step of controlling these feelings.

2(a): Thought

Jealousy can arise from faulty thinking which distorts our perception of reality. As Rabbi Dessler explains, "Jealousy happens when we focus on a few moments of success in someone else's life, and ignore their suffering."[78] As I mentioned previously, this is called "selective attention," where we focus on one aspect of a situation without viewing the whole picture.

> *There is an interesting example of selective attention regarding Bilam, the evil prophet. He was jealous of the Jewish people and wanted to curse them when they encamped in the desert before entering the Land of Israel. Bilam had only one eye, which is referred to as an evil eye, because it symbolized his distorted vision, which focused on the negative aspects of the Jewish People rather than viewing the whole picture.*[79]

To overcome jealousy, we need to become aware of our distorted thinking and to unmask the illusions it creates. One way to do this is to realize that however good another person's life seems, they also have their own set of challenges and hardships. I recall a Simon and Garfunkel song from my youth, called "Richard Cory," that illustrates this point.

The song is a ballad, sung from the perspective of a factory worker who worked for Richard Cory. The factory worker lived in poverty, hated his own life, and was envious of Cory, who enjoyed wealth, status, and popularity. Richard Cory was a person who was followed by the press and supported charities. The factory worker reflected that Richard must be very happy with everything he had, and he wished that he could be him. But the song ends on an unexpected note when we are told that Richard Cory went home one night and shot himself in the head.[80]

The reality of Richard Cory's life was radically different to the one perceived by the factory worker, and illustrates how far our perceptions can be from the truth.

Our selective attention may also cause us to ignore the positive things that we do have. Jewish thought asks the question, "Who is rich?"[81] One might think the answer would be someone who has an abundance of money — a multi-millionaire. The answer given, however, is "a person who appreciates what he has." This means that being truly rich is not a product of having great wealth but is a result of *appreciating* what one has. Internalizing this attitude and appreciating what we have helps us to reduce our jealousy.

> *Naomi was jealous of her sister Miriam. Miriam had a better job, a bigger house, and took expensive vacations — which Naomi could not afford. In therapy, Naomi started focusing on what she did have — a loving husband, happy children, and good health. She also reflected that Miriam's life was not one hundred percent perfect; she suffered from some chronic health issues which required frequent medical attention. Gaining a more balanced perspective helped Naomi reduce her jealousy toward her sister.*

2(b): Speech

Sharing jealous thoughts and feelings confidentially with a supportive person can also help us see through our irrational thought and overcome the self-defeating behavior which brought them about.

> *In therapy, Ben addressed the issue of his jealousy toward his wife, which was rooted in his experiences of rejection as a child. He shared in detail these early experiences and expressed the anger, sadness, and shame that he had experienced. This helped him to stop identifying himself with the shameful feelings and began to view himself in a more positive light. As a result, his self-esteem grew and his jealousy was reduced.*

Sometimes, when we are going through a difficult time, the process of expressing these emotions can bring great relief. In other situations, when another person is doing something that makes us jealous, it can be helpful to speak to them directly about it to try to improve the situation.

2(c): Action

Jealousy can be considered an internal communication which shows that a person is not fulfilled and wants more than he has. A typical counterproductive response is to try to overcome these feelings by "keeping up with the Joneses." This is never effective because if one catches up with the Joneses, he then discovers the Smiths, who have even more than the Joneses. There will always be someone who has more than he has.

Instead of trying to get more of what *others* have, we can use jealousy as a positive motivation to improve ourselves. As the Talmud teaches, "Jealousy between the Sages increases wisdom."[82] When the Sages felt jealous of each other's spiritual attainments, they used it to motivate themselves to study more and to become wiser. When we are jealous of others — by using it as an incentive to better ourselves — we become more fulfilled within ourselves and consequently less jealous.

> *Daniella, a full time mother, experienced jealousy when she encountered working mothers. In therapy,*

> *it became clear that her jealousy was based on her belief that she felt she had accomplished too little in her life. From a young age, she had dreamed about creating projects to help the poor but had lacked the motivation to do it. Now, Daniella used her jealousy to motivate herself to start to put her dreams into reality. She began to fundraise to help underprivileged children. These acts of altruism imbued her life with a greater sense of fulfillment and helped her to alleviate her jealousy.*

Giving to others and feeling responsible for them is particularly important in helping overcome jealousy, as it changes our focus from looking at others as competitors and threats to seeing them as friends who have their own needs.

> *Before my second child was born, my wife and I were concerned that our oldest child might feel jealous of the new baby. One piece of advice that we received was to give our eldest child a "job" as a helper to the new baby. She would have a new position of responsibility, and by giving to the baby she would not see him as a threat. Thank God it worked well.*

STAGE 3: TRANSFORMATION

In this stage, we go beyond reducing our jealousy to changing our nature so that we no longer begin to feel jealous in the first place. How can we accomplish this? We need to eliminate the self-destructive traits (e.g., laziness, lack of confidence) which are at the root of the jealousy and replace these with positive traits. As with all previous examples of transformation, this is achieved through repeating positive actions until new habits are formed.

> *At the end of the Cain and Abel episode, God placed a mark on Cain and made him a wanderer. There is an opinion that this "mark" was a gift of a dog. The reason Cain was given a dog was to help him learn the true nature of giving and gratitude, as dogs have a giving and loyal nature. This was the trait Cain needed to internalize in order to overcome his selfish and jealous nature.*[83]

When a person repeats acts of giving, he will, over time, become a more generous person. He will uproot the jealousy and free himself from it. He will then start to experience joy for the good fortune of others, instead of letting it diminish his happiness and create animosity.

A beautiful example of this is the relationship between Moses and his brother, Aaron. When Moses was chosen by God to lead the Jewish people out of Egypt, Aaron, who was Moses's older brother, could have easily felt overshadowed and been jealous of Moses that he was not chosen for this mission. But in fact, Aaron is described as having "joy in his heart,"[84] and was happy for Moses. God's appointment of Moses only increased Aaron's love for him. We, too, can find a new sense of joy and closeness to others when we transform our jealousy.

Exercise

Awareness

1. Identify times when you become jealous and recall the thoughts that go through your mind.
2. Do you have any self-defeating behaviors or traits that cause this jealousy?

Control

THOUGHT

3. Are you focusing on the short-term success of someone else without a perspective of the difficulties that they have faced?
4. Are you looking at the situation objectively, or ignoring what you have?

SPEECH

5. Share your feelings of jealousy with a supportive person and receive feedback.

ACTION

6. Make a plan of how you can overcome your jealousy by expressing yourself more fully.
7. Take action to help the person you feel jealous of.

Transformation

8. Repeat positive actions that help you to overcome the trait that is causing the jealousy — until you have created a new habit, and feel pleasure for the other's good fortune.

Chapter 9

Love, Relationships, and Marriage

*When our love was strong, my wife and I could have slept
on the blade of a sword. Now our love has grown weak,
a bed sixty cubits wide isn't large enough.*

(Talmud, *Sanhedrin* 7a)

ONE of the greatest problems in society today is unhappy marriages, with a divorce rate of fifty percent, or higher, in many Western countries.[85] Even many marriages that do not end in divorce are often far from ideal. But it is not only marriages where problems lie; difficult relationships with family members, friends, and work associates can also cause untold grief.

In this section, we will look at how to build loving relationships. We will focus mainly on marriage relationships but these principles and approaches can be applied to help improve all relationships.

STAGE 1: AWARENESS

The first step in creating good relationships is to understand the relationship dynamics and source of any underlying problems. Let's look, for example, at one of the most common problems in marriage, that of "falling out of love."

Many of these relationships begin on a high, with a couple becoming infatuated with each other. They may have felt that they have met the person of their dreams, who will fulfill all of their unmet needs. But infatuation is not true love, and develops from the projection of positive qualities onto another person, which blinds us from seeing their faults.

When the initial high begins to fade, the true person is revealed — warts and all. Negative traits may then begin to cause antagonism, and it is common for power struggles to develop in which each person strives to have their needs met. Shaming and blaming often follows, where each person lashes out at the other's insecurities causing arguments to spiral out of control. The relationship we once thought was the answer to our dreams now becomes a living nightmare.

> *David and Ruth became enamored with each other when they first met. David was charming and sincere; Ruth was kind and sweet. Ruth was the first person that David felt he could truly open up to, and Ruth felt deeply appreciated by David.*
>
> *A few months after they were married, David started to become less attentive and caring toward Ruth. Ruth thought that she had done something wrong and began to pressure David into spending more time with her. David reacted to this by backing off. Ruth then felt even more unappreciated and responded by becoming highly critical. Arguments flared up with increasing regularity until they were a daily occurrence.*
>
> *In therapy, it became clear that the source of their problems developed from the fact that David had always been a loner and was used to spending much of his time by himself. The excitement of courtship and the early stages of marriage had created a temporary distraction, but after a few months of marriage, he began to feel a deep need to spend more time alone.*

> *David's actions triggered Ruth's insecurities, as she took them as signs of rejection.*

Looking a bit deeper into relationships often reveals that the root of conflict lies in patterns of behavior that began in childhood, such as a lack of ability to trust or a desire to control. Attachment theory describes three childhood styles of behavior: secure, anxious, and avoidant.[86] Secure individuals find it relatively easy to become close to others. Anxious people are more aggressive and needy in their pursuit of affection, and avoidant ones tend to withdraw and avoid conflict.

> *David had an avoidant style as he had become a loner in childhood to protect himself from the hurt of critical parents. Ruth had an anxious style, as her father abandoned her and her mother when she was young. To protect herself from future rejection, she developed the tendency to be aggressive and critical.*

Thus far, I have focused on one common example, but there are many other relationship dynamics that cause problems. For example, some couples may gradually become less enamored with each other without major fights until their marriage becomes empty and loveless. Whatever the case, the first step is to gain insight into the dynamics and the source of problems within the relationship.

STAGE 2: CONTROL

Once we gain a greater awareness of the dynamics in the relationship, we can begin to improve the relationship.

2(a): Thought

When we feel negatively toward someone, we tend to justify the feeling with compelling reasons. "He is so selfish/inconsiderate/

rude!" Cognitive therapy points out that our reasoning often results from distorted thinking; we may jump to the wrong conclu-
sions, see things in all-or-nothing terms, or fail to view the whole
picture correctly.

We may also project our own negative feelings about ourselves
or others onto the "disliked person." We hate in others what we
hate in ourselves. As the Talmud teaches, "When one disqualifies
another person, he is really doing so due to possessing that same
trait (blemish)."[87]

To improve the relationship, we need
to see through these irrational thoughts
and projections by trying to understand
the other person and his perspective.
As the psychologist Erich Fromm wrote,
"Try to see the difference between my
picture of a person and his behavior as
it is narcissistically distorted and the
person's reality as it exists regardless of my interests, needs,
and fears."[88]

> "When one disqualifies another person, he is really doing so due to possessing that same trait (blemish)."

This understanding helps a person to become less reactive and
more compassionate.

> *When David realized that Ruth's criticism was
> rooted in a fear of abandonment due to her childhood
> experience, he took it less personally and began to
> withdraw less. Similarly, when Ruth understood that
> David's habit of withdrawing was his way of dealing
> with critical parents (which had carried over to their
> relationship), she began to feel less rejected and, in
> turn, became less critical of him.*

Imago relationship therapy teaches that it is common for people to subconsciously be drawn to choose spouses who exhibit
the same difficult behavior patterns as their parents, or to project

onto their spouses these behavior patterns.[89] Understanding how pain from past relationships can be projected onto current ones also helps to reduce the current conflict. We then begin to realize that the upset that we are experiencing is not wholly due to the current relationship, but from experiences in our past.

> *Ruth realized that David's withdrawal from the relationship was so painful to her because it reminded her of her father abandoning the family, and David realized that Ruth's criticisms hurt so much because they reminded him of his critical parents. These realizations helped them feel less offended by each other's actions as they understood that they were magnified by their past experiences.*

2(b): Speech

Building healthy communication also plays a vital role in improving relationships. As King Solomon taught: "Death and life are in the hands of the tongue."[90]

It is not just openly aggressive communication that causes harm. Untold anguish can also result from passive-aggressive communication (in which dissatisfaction is expressed indirectly) and avoidant communication (in which difficult issues are "swept under the rug").

> "Death and life are in the hands of the tongue."

To break out of these negative forms of communication and create a safe environment where one can discuss issues productively, the following techniques can be very effective.

1. **Beginning communication in a calm and positive way**

   Dr. John Gottman, professor emeritus of psychology at Washington University, has carried out extensive research on marital relationships. He explains that ninety-six per cent of the time, he can predict the fate of a conflict discussion in the opening three minutes of watching a couple, as discussions invariably end on the same note on which they began.[91]

   Therefore, a couple should find a good time to talk — when both parties are in a calm and collected state of mind and there are no other people around. It is a good idea to begin on a positive note; for instance, one person should acknowledge the other person's point of view or apologize for that which he or she may have done incorrectly. Rabbi Salanter taught that at a time of giving criticism, we should be particularly careful to show the other person a great deal of respect.[92]

2. **Using mirroring to avoid insulting and/or demanding remarks**

   The Talmud records numerous arguments between students of the respective schools of Hillel and Shammai.

It says that a Heavenly voice declared that decisions should follow the opinions of the school of Hillel. What is the reasoning behind this? Surely the school of Shammai had great Sages as well?! The difference lay in how they related to each other. The students of the school of Hillel were deemed to be superior because they chose to speak patiently and consider and restate the opinions of the school of Shammai before explaining their own.[93]

A similar approach, used in Imago relationship therapy, is known as "mirroring," in which each person paraphrases the other's opinion before expressing his own.[94] Opinions also are expressed by using "I" statements reflecting how one feels, rather than with accusatory statements that begin with "you." For example, instead of saying "You're so selfish — you always leave a mess for me to clean up," one says, "I feel upset when I have to clean up after you." This places the focus on the way the speaker feels about the other's behavior, rather than identifying the other with his mistake, which can cause the person to feel attacked and to become defensive.

In therapy, David and Ruth used mirroring to help them speak about their issues.

Ruth: I feel quite hurt when you come home and spend the whole evening reading or looking at your computer rather than spending time together with me.

David: It hurts you when I come home and spend the evening reading or on my computer and we don't spend time together. Did I understand you correctly?

Ruth: Yes.

David: Is there anything else you would like to say?

Ruth (starting to cry): Yes, it reminds me of my Dad, who never wanted to spend time with me.

David: It's hurtful when I come home and don't spend time with you because it reminds you of your father not wanting to spend time with you.
Ruth: Yes.

Through the mirroring, instead of becoming reactive and defensive, David began to understand Ruth's feelings more deeply. When Ruth mirrored David's concerns, he also felt understood. They then felt for the first time that they could begin to communicate about these issues in an open and safe way.

3. **Employing validation, empathy, and behavior change requests**

Carl Rogers, the originator of person-centered therapy, explained that listening requires that we enter another person's world and experience his feelings sensitively and accurately, as if they were our own.[95] When this takes place, the listener goes beyond the words being expressed, and empathy and understanding begin.

Imago relationship therapy emphasizes the importance of the listener validating the speaker by explaining that he understands what was said and that it makes sense from the speaker's perspective. It also encourages him to empathize with the speaker by expressing how he imagines the speaker must be feeling.[96]

In the case of David and Ruth:
David: It makes sense to me that you get upset when I come home and don't spend time with you, and that is compounded by the fact that it reminds you of what your father used to do.
Ruth: Yes.
David: It must make you feel rejected and undervalued.
Ruth: That's exactly how I feel.

When we feel understood, it has a calming effect and creates an empathetic environment in which people can work together to resolve their differences.

We can also make requests for a change in the other person's behavior to help resolve conflicts. For example:

> *Ruth: Maybe I can suggest we spend twenty minutes at the end of an evening to connect?*
> *David: Okay, that's fine with me.*

4. **Using positive language**

While on the topic of speech it is also important to mention the value of making sincere positive statements, such as words of gratitude and affection, and the power they have to improve relationships. As Rabbi Moses ibn Ezra wrote. "Words that come from the heart enter the heart."[97]

> *I was once on a crowded bus in Jerusalem when I saw, standing on the other side of the bus, Rabbi Moshe Aaron Stern, who was well known for his wise marital advice. Not wanting to squander the opportunity, I squeezed through the crowded bus and asked him if he could give me some advice for creating a happy marriage. He said, "If you want to get three A's in marriage, be sure to give your wife plenty of attention, affection, and appreciation. Attention — by making time to listen to each other every day, Affection — by expressing warmth, and Appreciation — by expressing gratitude."*

> "Words that come from the heart enter the heart."

2(c): Action

Taking action is another powerful way to improve relationships. Couple therapists often suggest increasing acts of care and giving, either in small steps, such as giving a little gift or having a weekly "date" night, or larger ones such as taking short trips away to spend quality time together and reconnect.

Rabbi Dessler explained how this works. The Hebrew word for love, *ahavah*, is derived from the word *hav*, to give, since we develop loving relationships by giving. This is because a person loves a person to whom he gives or provides nurturing.[98]

> *The Talmud illustrates this concept when discussing the case of a person who sees two donkeys, each carrying a heavy load. One donkey is owned by a friend and the other by someone toward whom he has bad feelings. The Talmud asks, "Who should the person help first?" The answer is that it should be the donkey belonging to the person he does not like. This is because by giving to that person he will not only help him with his donkey, but also improve their relationship by giving to him.*[99]

Giving is most effective when it comes from a place of care and is a response to another person's true needs. I am certain that almost everyone has experienced the difference; think about how you feel when you receive a present which you felt the giver really thought you would appreciate, as opposed to one which you are sure was purchased in haste and merely out of convenience. This is especially important as many conflicts arise from struggles to have unmet needs fulfilled.

> *David and Ruth improved their relationship by trying to meet each other's needs. David spent more quality time with Ruth, and Ruth gave David plenty of time to be alone. They stopped fighting and began to appreciate each other more.*

King Solomon stated, "Just as water reflects the face of man, so too the heart reflects the heart of another."[100] This means that the way a person acts toward another is reflected back to him in the way the other person acts toward him. When one person starts acting in a more caring way, the other reciprocates, which creates an upward spiral of affection and love.

This, in turn, builds a fulfilling bond of love as well as sanctity in the relationship. The Talmud says, "When a man and wife act fittingly toward each other, God's presence dwells between them."[101] The following story illustrates how giving helps create a deep bond of love and closeness to God.

> *There is a legend that the place where the Temple in Jerusalem was built had originally been owned by a man with two sons. One son was married with a large family, while the other lived alone. When the father died, the brothers split the land and lived on it side by side. The single brother felt sorry for his brother, as he had a large family to support. He decided to get up in the middle of the night and throw a barrel of wheat over the fence to his brother's side so that his brother would have more to sell. The brother with the large family felt sorry for his single brother, as all he had was the land and no children to help him work it. So he decided to get up in the middle of the night and throw a barrel of wheat over the fence. They continued in this way every night for years. Somehow, every morning each had the same amount of wheat.*
>
> *One night, when they were both carrying their barrels of wheat to throw over, they saw each other and immediately understood what had been happening all those years. They threw down their barrels, ran toward each other and hugged and kissed. God, looking down on them, said, "In this place of such profound love I*

want my presence to dwell," and God then established this place for the building of the Temple.[102]

The building of strong and sanctified relationships also results from sharing a sense of meaning and mutual spiritual advancement. We will look at the importance of these factors in greater depth in Chapters 11 and 12, when we discuss meaning and spirituality.

STAGE 3: TRANSFORMATION

The goal of a married couple is to "become one flesh,"[103] to create a oneness in which each loves and cares so deeply for the other that it is as if they were one person.

> *Rabbi Aryeh Levin, who lived in Jerusalem in the mid-twentieth century, was known as the Tzaddik (Saint) of Jerusalem for the work he did on behalf of the sick and poor. One time, he accompanied his wife to the doctor as she was experiencing pain in her leg. When the doctor asked what the problem was, Rabbi Levin answered, "My wife's leg is hurting us."*[104]

This type of loving bond develops through repeated acts of giving and caring. To achieve this, a person may have to go beyond character traits that could otherwise hold him back, such as being controlling, self-centered, or overly needy.

> *David and Ruth created a deep and loving bond by repeatedly meeting each other's needs. David spent more time with Ruth and became less of a loner. Ruth gave David time to be alone, and in doing so conquered her fear of abandonment. By making these changes, not only did they transform their relationship, but they changed their own personalities,*

resolving their unhealthy coping behaviors from their respective pasts.

Difficulties in relationships, especially in marriage, can therefore have a hidden purpose. Relationships are a place of healing, as they bring both an awareness of our shortcomings and the motivation to transform them in order to create truly loving bonds with others.

Relationship Growth Chart

Discover source
of relationship issue

Awareness

Stop negative projections
and thinking

Control: thought

Communicate
effectively

Control: speech

Meet each other's needs
and do caring actions

Control: action

Grow as a person
and form a strong, loving bond

Transformation

Exercise

Awareness

1. Think of a relationship you want to improve. Which problems in the relationship do you wish to improve? What are the underlying dynamics of the relationship?
2. Identify any underlying habits or negative traits that lie at the root of your relationship issues.

Control

THOUGHT

3. Look at the situation from the other's perspective and understand how you may be projecting negative attitudes onto them.

SPEECH

4. Communicate with them about difficulties in the relationship by:
   A. Starting in a positive and calm way.
   B. Mirroring.
   C. Validating, showing empathy, and making simple requests.
5. Share one thing you appreciate about the other person.

ACTION

6. Write a list of three to five things which you believe the other person would appreciate you doing for them; then put them into action.

Transformation

7. Repeat positive actions of giving, overcoming the negative traits that have held you back before, which are at the root of your relationship issues.

Section C:

Spirituality

Chapter 10

Overcoming Guilt and Achieving Moral Integrity

Don't judge yourself as a bad person.

(Ethics of the Fathers 2:18)

WE all have times when we feel guilty, whether about a small matter, such as forgetting to return a borrowed object, or a larger issue, where we fall far below that which we expect from ourselves. Guilt is rooted in the struggle between the true self (our conscience) and the deceptive self. When we follow our conscience we maintain our integrity; when we succumb to the rationalizations created by the deceptive self, we lose credibility with ourselves and guilt develops.

There have been many psychological experiments which examine people's ability to follow their moral conscience when placed under pressure. One famous experiment, known as the Milgram Experiment, was conducted at Yale University in July 1961.

> *Volunteers were asked to play the role of a teacher to a student who was in another room. A man in a white coat gave the volunteers their instructions.*
>
> *If the student made a mistake, they were told to press a button that administered an electric shock to*

the student. The volunteers were unaware that the student was an actor who pretended to feel the shocks and scream out in pain, but in reality felt nothing. With each mistake, the volunteers were urged to press a button that administered increasing levels of electric voltage. This research was aimed at discovering at which point the volunteers would refuse to continue participating in the experiment. The results showed that more than sixty percent of volunteers continued to press the button, issuing shocks of 450 volts, which would have been fatal to the student.[105]

Fortunately, there are many other examples which demonstrate people's ability to follow their conscience under adverse conditions. One of my favorites is the heroic actions of Chiune Sugihara in World War II:

Chiune Sugihara was a diplomat in the Japanese consul in Vilna, Lithuania, during the 1940s. Jews living there were desperate to obtain travel visas to escape the threat of a German invasion. Sugihara was instructed by his superiors not to issue any visas. He knew that the plight of thousands of Jewish lives were in his hands, but if he disobeyed orders he would endanger his own career and the safety of his family. Sugihara made a decision to disobey his orders. Supported by his wife, he worked eighteen to twenty hour days issuing thousands of visas. He wrote, "I followed my own conscience and listened to it." As a result of his decision, he saved six thousand lives including the entire Mir Yeshiva (college of Jewish studies). Japan was infuriated by his actions and ended Sugihara's public service career in 1947, sending Sugihara and his family into poverty. In 1984, Yad Vashem, the Holocaust Memorial Museum in

Jerusalem, recognized Chiune Sugihara with the award of being one of the "Righteous among the Nations."[106]

When we ignore our conscience, guilt emerges as a form of self-condemnation. There are times when this guilt may act as a positive motivation for change. But often, it results in what can be called unhealthy guilt, or "toxic guilt," which is when we ruminate over our mistakes as a form of self-punishment without any change occurring. Toxic guilt can cause considerable psychological suffering such as depression, anxiety, and low self-esteem.

A person may also find that this guilt causes him to become trapped in a cycle of self-destructive behavior (illustrated below). For example, a person who feels depressed may go to the fridge and indulge in "comfort food" as a coping strategy in an effort to feel better. This may give initial relief but often leads to feelings of shame and guilt about the overeating. This guilt then causes the person to become more depressed, which leads to more comfort eating.

"I don't feel good"

Coping Strategies
Overeating

Guilt and Shame

Short-Term Relief
Through giving
into the desires

To restore our moral integrity and overcome guilt, Judaism teaches a process of *teshuvah*. This is often translated as "repentance," but more accurately, it means "to return" (derived from the word *shuv*), and refers to the process by which we can return to our true selves.

Teshuvah begins with recognizing and accepting responsibility for a mistake. Once recognized, there are four further principal steps:[107]

1. Regretting the mistake
2. Refraining from making the mistake
3. Sharing verbally with God the mistake and the regret
4. Resolving not to repeat the mistake in the future

A person can also do *teshuvah* on the character traits that are behind their improper actions.

There are clear parallels between the *teshuvah* process and the ACTive method.

1. Awareness corresponds to the first step of *teshuvah*, in which we recognize and accept our mistake.
2. Control occurs through regretting, ceasing to do the mistake, verbally sharing the mistake with God, and resolving to avoid the mistake in the future.
3. Transformation occurs when we change the underlying character traits that caused the mistake, thereby uprooting the urge to repeat it again.

Let's examine this in greater depth.

STAGE 1: AWARENESS

The first stage of change is to attain an honest and accurate awareness of the mistake and its causes, and to accept responsibility for it. To achieve this, we may have to overcome a desire to deny the mistake or blame it on others.

> *When Adam went into hiding after eating from the Tree of Knowledge, God asked him, "Where are you?" The commentator Rashi explains that God asked this question in order to give Adam the opportunity to admit his mistake and to do teshuvah. Adam failed to grasp this opportunity and went on to blame Eve, saying, "The woman whom you gave me, she gave me from the tree, and I ate."[108]*

In marital therapy, both parties will often initially blame their problems on each other. Gradually, if the counseling is to be successful, each partner needs to become aware of his or her own role in harming the relationship and to accept responsibility for it.

One factor that contributes to the tendency to deny a mistake is that the more a mistake is repeated, the less sensitive a person becomes to the mistake. As the Talmud says, "Once a person makes a mistake and repeats it, it becomes to him as though it was permitted."[109]

While some people regress into denial, others show the opposite tendency, known as "turning against self." They assume too much responsibility and experience an over-exaggerated sense of guilt. This tendency can develop as a result of being made to feel overly guilty in childhood by authority figures or cultural influences.

We need to gain an accurate perspective, otherwise we may find it too overwhelming to change. One effective method to achieve this is to use a thought diary.

> *Carol, mother of three, was extremely devoted to her children; nevertheless, she always believed that she wasn't doing enough for them. She was disorganized at times, and one day she arrived very late to pick up her six-year-old daughter Jenny from school. When Carol arrived, Jenny was crying hysterically. Jenny*

said, "I thought you were late because you had been killed in a car crash." Carol felt terrible and she feared that she may have caused her daughter permanent psychological damage. She was overcome by guilt. Later that day, Carol used a thought diary to help her deal with her feelings.

Situation	Self-critical Thoughts	Evidence Supporting Negative Thoughts	Evidence Against Negative Thoughts	Alternative Perspective
I picked up my daughter late from school.	I am a terrible mother because I was late to pick up my daughter.	My daughter was crying. My daughter said she was scared that I had been killed.	I very rarely come late. I am devoted to my children's needs and generally put them before my own.	I am a caring mother who makes occasional mistakes.

Filling out the thought diary helped Carol to understand that thinking of herself as a bad mother was far from the truth, and that in reality, she was a caring mother who at times made mistakes.

Once we have accurately recognized our mistake, it is important to understand *why* it occurred. We may have been fooled into it by our self-deceptive thoughts with promises of pleasure and fulfillment. There are other times when a deeper psychological explanation comes into play and we follow our self-deceptive thinking to make up for a lacking or inner pain from our youth.

- *As an adolescent, Rebecca would get a thrill from shoplifting in expensive department stores. In therapy, she understood that the roots of her tendency to shoplift came as a consequence of growing up in a poor home where she was never able to afford the things that her friends from more affluent families took for granted.*

- *Jacob turned to internet addictions to overcome his feelings of emptiness and depression. The original source of these feelings arose from a lack of meaningful relationships and activity in his life that started in his youth.*

STAGE 2: CONTROL

In the control stage, we learn to hold ourselves back from the urge to repeat our mistakes. For example, a man who has been promiscuous and then finds himself in the same situation and experiencing similar urges as before is now able to resist these urges and not repeat his mistake.[110]

2(a): Thought

When we make a mistake, there is a tendency to identify ourselves with the mistake, and feel toxic guilt — we think of ourselves as bad or shameful. This can create a feeling of despair — why should we try to improve if we are good for nothing?

To move beyond toxic guilt, we need to distinguish between the two parts of our being — the true self (which is inherently good) and our actions, which mistakenly followed the deceptive self. In this way we can maintain a sense of positivity about ourselves and regret only our actions, and we will be motivated to change.

Rav Yehuda taught that we should "calculate the gain of a mistake against its loss" as a motivation to stop making mistakes.[111] Many therapies use this approach to motivate clients to change self-defeating behaviors. In cognitive therapy it is called a "cost-benefit analysis,"[112] which involves a person weighing the pros and cons of his behavior. This is important because very often, a person gains a payoff, a short-term benefit from counter-productive behavior. This often occurs on a subconscious level and lures him back to repeating the said behavior.

> *Rebecca experienced both a short-term high from shoplifting and an escape from her negative feelings. However, one time she was caught by a security guard and let off with a warning. This shocked her and made her reflect on the potential damage that shoplifting could have on her life. She then realized it was not worth the risk and she became motivated to change.*

2(b): Speech

Unburdening our shameful and guilty feelings to a supportive person also helps us to relieve feelings of toxic guilt. These emotions are often guarded like a secret, but when expressed, they become normalized.

> *A key to helping Jacob overcome his internet addiction was speaking in detail about it. This included which sites he visited, how much time he spent online, and what exactly he hoped to gain from doing so. This communication reduced the hidden shame he was carrying which had been perpetuating his behavior.*

Speaking openly and candidly about the history of addictions to other group members is also one of the first steps an Alcoholics Anonymous (AA) member takes in his pursuit of change.

In cases when the behavior is rooted in pain from the past, talking about other emotions associated with it, such as anger and despair (as discussed earlier), is also very important.

After reducing the toxic guilt, speaking with others can help us to find true remorse by reflecting on the consequences of our actions. The Talmud relates the story of Elazar ben Durdiya which demonstrates that even unexpected comments from others can bring remorse, and that no matter how far we fall, there is always hope.

> *There wasn't a prostitute in the world whom Elazar ben Durdiya had not encountered. Once he heard of a prostitute who lived far away. He traveled the seven seas and paid a great sum of money for her services. When he was involved with her, he passed wind. She remarked, "Just like that air will never return to its source, so too your teshuvah will never be accepted." He was suddenly struck by a deep sense of remorse over his actions and began to cry. This led him to regret his past misdeeds and to perform teshuvah. When his soul left his body, a Heavenly voice called out, "Welcome Rabbi Elazar Ben Durdiya to the World to Come."[13]*

2(c): Action

Once a person experiences remorse, the next step is to make a decision to stop repeating the undesired behavior in the future. Because one still has the urge to repeat the mistake at this stage, it is important that even after making the decision he should try to avoid situations where he may be tempted to repeat it.

- *Rebecca avoided going into very expensive stores where she would feel tempted to steal.*
- *Jacob put special internet blocks on his computer to prevent him from accessing undesirable sites.*

If we have made mistakes involving harm to others, the decision to change should be followed by a sincere request for forgiveness from those who have been hurt by our actions. Judaism is often mistakenly portrayed as a vengeful religion teaching a literal understanding of "an eye for eye"; in reality, it stresses the importance of forgiving those who sincerely regret their actions.

A similar process to this takes place in AA, where people construct a moral inventory of people they have harmed and attempt to make amends with them. Forgiving and being forgiven has a liberating effect, dissolving feelings of anger, bitterness, guilt, and the desire for revenge. With forgiveness, there emerges a sense of peace with our past and a joy in the present.

One reason for this is that on a spiritual level, when we ignore our conscience, we also break our connection with God. To restore this spiritual connection, we ask forgiveness from God. This is one reason why Yom Kippur, the Day of Atonement — a day devoted to *teshuvah* — is considered a joyful day rather than a sad or depressing one. It rebuilds and renews relationships with the true self, others, and God.

STAGE 3: TRANSFORMATION

In the Transformation stage, we go beyond resisting the urge to repeat our negative behavior, and change our nature so that we no longer retain the desire to repeat it. As with other forms of transformation, we repeat positive acts until a new habit is formed.

> *Rebecca gradually stopped stealing after reflecting on the consequences of her actions. She then resolved to be honest in all her dealings, exercising extreme caution until this became second nature. She then began to take pleasure in being honest and no longer had a desire to steal.*

These new habits create a positive moral force, which now imbues life with an inner sense of integrity, joy and peace of mind.

Exercise

Awareness

1. Make a list of three to five mistakes you have made. Choose one to work on.
2. Understand the cause of the mistake and identify if there is an underlying trait at its root.

Control

THOUGHT

3. Regret the mistake by thinking about its negative consequences compared to what you're gaining from it.

SPEECH

4. Share with a supportive person the guilty thoughts and feelings you may have about the mistake, as well as your regrets.
5. Make sincere apologizes to anyone you may have hurt through it and ask for their forgiveness.
6. Share with God your mistake, regrets, and decision to change.

ACTION

7. Make a decision to stop, and avoid situations that would tempt you to repeat it.

Transformation

8. Repeat positive actions that will help you uproot the trait that underlies your mistake, and create a new positive habit.

Chapter 11

Meaning and Purpose

If I am not for myself, who will be for me? But if I am only for myself, what am I? And if not now, when?

(Ethics of the Fathers 1:14)

WE all have a drive to express ourselves in a meaningful way, to make the world a better place — *to make a difference.* Jewish thought teaches that everyone has a unique role to play, and that one should view the world as their own personal responsibility. As the Talmud explains, a person is obligated to say, "the world was created for me,"[114] which means the world is my responsibility.

One of the reasons why Kaddish, the mourner's prayer, is said for a person who passes away is that there is something missing in the world without his or her unique contribution. Kaddish reminds and motivates the congregation to draw inspiration from the life of the deceased in order to fill that gap.[115]

Victor Frankl, an existential psychotherapist and Holocaust survivor, proposed that the drive for meaning is mankind's primary motivation. While in Auschwitz, he observed that fellow prisoners who had a sense of purpose showed a greater propensity for survival. He expressed a similar sentiment to that

"Everyone has his own specific vocation or mission in life. He cannot be replaced, nor can his life be repeated, thus everyone's task is unique as his specific opportunity."

held by Jewish thought. "Everyone has his own specific vocation or mission in life. He cannot be replaced, nor can his life be repeated, thus everyone's task is unique as his specific opportunity."[116]

But when we don't express our talents in a purposeful way, inner turmoil results; this can cause psychological problems such as anxiety, depression, and low self-esteem.

> *A story is told of Reb Zusha, a great Chassidic master. One day, his students found him crying. "Why are you crying?" they asked. He answered, "When I die, God won't ask me why weren't you Abraham, Isaac, or Jacob, but I will be asked, why weren't you Zusha?!"*

Victor Frankl explained that without a sense of purpose, a person will feel an emptiness, an existential vacuum. He gives the example of someone who has free time on the weekend and experiences a void, as he becomes aware of the lack of content in his life.[117] This experience is also common at birthdays, New Year's Day, and times of life transitions.

> *I remember feeling this "void" soon after finishing high school. I was storing away all my books and notes from my school years in a large suitcase and putting them into the back of a wardrobe. As I lifted the suitcase a scary thought crossed my mind. "What am I doing all this for? I'm planning to go on to university to study for my future career then hopefully get married, have a family, work for thirty years and that's it?!" At that moment, I felt a deep sense of emptiness.*

Midlife crises, a lack of fulfillment at work, and the empty nest syndrome can also be manifestations of the pain of a lack of purpose. When the renowned psychiatrist Carl Jung experienced an acute midlife crisis, it prompted him to develop theories which proposed that the passage through midlife is a spiritual or religious journey, and embodies a search for a deeper meaning, value, and purpose in life.[118]

Although modern psychotherapy and Jewish philosophy recognize the drive for meaning, Jewish thought explains that man is not merely looking to express himself more meaningfully in something he creates, but is in search of ultimate meaning, our true purpose in life.

We are now going to look at how we express our drive for meaning, and how this alleviates psychological suffering.

Stage 1: Awareness

To begin, we need to gain awareness into our drive for meaning and what is holding us back from expressing it more deeply. Let's look at a few common examples.

Rabbi Luzzatto explained that people avoid facing the deeper issues of life, such as expressing themselves more meaningfully, by keeping themselves so busy that they never have the time to think about such things.[119] Frankl described this phenomena as "an unheard cry for meaning,"[120] wherein people mask their inner void by pursuing power, status, material success, and physical pleasure. He also explained that, "Existential frustration often eventuates in sexual compensation. We can observe in such cases that the sexual libido becomes rampant in the existential vacuum."[121]

Laziness can also play a role in creating an inertia that prevents us from pursuing a more meaningful life. We may think, "Why should I bother to strive to contribute more?" As King Solomon said, the lazy person invents many rationalizations. As he wrote in Proverbs, "The lazy man rationalizes, saying, 'There is a lion on the road, a lion is on the highways,' as an excuse not to travel to study from his teacher."[122]

Fear, worry, and a lack of self-confidence are other causes, which may have their roots in the person's upbringing. A child who receives critical feedback and discouragement about his aspirations and abilities may then lack the confidence to pursue his dreams and goals later in life.

> *Aaron, a tax lawyer, had a loving family and was well-respected by his peers. At the age of forty, he started to gamble and drink. After losing large sums of money, he decided to enter therapy. Aaron discovered that although he appeared to be externally happy, he was unfulfilled. His unhappiness was rooted in the fact that he found his work very boring and that he had never wanted to go into law in the first place. As a child, he possessed a strong sense of social justice and wanted to become a social worker. But he was ridiculed by his parents who didn't consider it a sufficiently well-paid and prestigious job for their son. As a result of this ridicule, Aaron developed a terrible fear of doing things that would bring him ridicule from others, and he ignored his desire to become a social worker.*

It's not just individual criticism that can inhibit a person, but social pressure from prevailing attitudes in society also play a role. In Western society, the very desire to understand the meaning of life or one's own purpose is frequently seen as something utterly irrelevant.

Once we have become aware of what is holding us back, we can move on to the stage of control, where we look at how to overcome the obstacles to expressing our drive for meaning.

Stage 2: Control

2(a): Thought

Taking time to introspect and to think about these issues is an important way to move forward. The great *mussar* teachers

recommend setting aside daily and weekly times for soul search-
ing and contemplation, known in Hebrew as *cheshbon hanefesh*.
Rabbi Luzzatto writes that just as a businessman sets aside
regular times to evaluate if his business is succeeding and how it
can be improved, we too should set aside regular times to introspect and evaluate our own lives.[123]

Here are a few important questions that might be helpful
to contemplate.

1. What are my dreams, aspirations, and passions?
2. In which way could I more fully express my talents to
   benefit others?
3. What is the meaning of life?

Rabbi Noah Weinberg, *zt"l*, was fond of asking people two other
questions to focus their attentions on addressing these issues.
"Are you eating to live or living to eat?" People would answer ada-
mantly, "Eating to live!" He would then reply, "If you are eating to
live, what you are *living* for?"

He would also ask, "Do you know what you are willing to die
for?" And then continue, "If you don't know what you are willing to die for, you haven't begun to live, and if you do know, live
for it!"[124]

Reflecting on the preciousness of
life and our mortality can also help us
to track down the things which mean
the most to us (without becoming too
morbid). This sentiment is expressed in
Ecclesiastes: "It is better to go to a house
of mourning than a wedding,"[125] because the experience of going to a house of mourning causes a person to reflect on his life
and improve himself.

> "It is better to go to
> a house of mourning
> than a wedding."

Irvin Yalom, an existential psychiatrist and writer, explained
that thinking about death can cause terror. He described the

phenomenon known as "death anxiety," when a person tries to cope with the inevitability of death by denial of its reality. He explains, however, that the recognition of death is a factor that helps transform our lives and can actually be the source of zest and creativity. Stated dramatically, he writes, "The idea of death saves us."[126]

Let's look at a few varied examples of how thinking about mortality has helped people.

- *There was once a merchant who used to attend synagogue in the morning to pray, study afterward, and then leave for work. However, with the pressures of life, he slowly reduced his studying until he abandoned it completely. One morning he noticed that his hair was beginning to turn gray, and he realized that his days were numbered. The shock he experienced that morning motivated him to stay in synagogue after praying and to learn for a couple of hours. By the time he arrived at his store, his wife had become frantic; she believed that his absence was causing them to lose customers. The merchant said to his wife, "If I was already dead I wouldn't be able to come to the store. Each day, let's imagine, for a couple of hours, that I have already died — this way I will be able to study every day."[127]*
- *Alfred Nobel, inventor of dynamite, was born in Stockholm, Sweden, in 1833. In 1888, he was astonished to read his own obituary, which was headlined, "The Merchant of Death Is Dead." Nobel's brother, Ludvig, had actually died and the paper had confused the two brothers. The article disturbed Nobel greatly, causing him to think about the things that he had accomplished in his life and*

for which he would be remembered. This inspired him to make changes to his will. He established the Nobel Prizes, leaving his fortune to be used to create a series of prizes for those who had conferred the "greatest benefit" upon mankind.[128]

- *At the age of seventy–two, Kirk Douglas, one of Hollywood's most famous actors, was in a helicopter crash. Two people died, and he sustained severe injuries. As he lay in the hospital recovering, he was haunted by the tragedy. It led him in a search to discover the meaning of life, why we are here, and the nature of God. In his search for the meaning of life, he discovered and learned more about his Jewish identity and Judaism.*[129]

2(b): Speech

Expressing our thoughts is another powerful tool to help us deepen our sense of purpose and is one of the reasons that people seek psychotherapy.

Therapy provides a non-critical environment in which to examine these issues and to explore many of the questions listed above, such as, "What are my hopes, dreams, and aspirations?" "What is my life's purpose?" "How do I want to use my life to contribute to others?"

A person can also explore the experiences and messages he received when he was young which may be holding him back. Gestalt Therapy, for example, uses an imagery technique to help people resolve negative experiences and messages from their past. Let's look at how it helped Aaron resolve the issues from his past.

Aaron imagined the time when he was being ridiculed by his father for wanting to become a social worker. He recalled the following conversation:

Aaron: I remember a time when I was fourteen and my father asked me what I wanted to do when I grew up.

Therapist: What happened then?

Aaron: I said, "I would like to become a social worker like my Aunt Judith." And my father started laughing and saying, "You'll never be able to support a family on her salary — I have not worked this hard for you to turn into a nobody!"

Therapist: How did you feel?

Aaron: I felt embarrassed and humiliated.

Therapist: What would you like to have said at the time?

Aaron: I feel too scared to say anything.

Therapist: Give it a try.

Aaron: I wish you would not laugh at me. It makes me feel so humiliated. What I really want to do is to help people and I have no interest in becoming a lawyer. I don't care about having a lower standard of living; what is important to me is to use my life to make a difference to other people.

After Aaron expressed his upset and disagreement, he went on, in therapy, to understand his father's point of view and to forgive him. Aaron was subsequently able to find the internal strength to reach beyond his fear of ridicule. He decided to begin to use his expertise as a lawyer to assist victims of abuse. This gave his life a deeper sense of meaning.

Communicating with a supportive non-professional can also be very powerful.

When I first thought about leaving my work in Jewish education I was uncertain of my next step, so I discussed it with a friend. He asked me the following

question, "If you could do anything with your life, what
would you really want to do?"

"I would like to grow as a person both emotionally
and spiritually, and work with others, one-on-one and
in groups, to help them grow as well." I replied.

My friend then said, "So why don't you do that?"
This question scared me to the core. It was my dream,
but what right did I have to think I could, or even
should, try to achieve it?

This conversation was important in leading me to follow my
dreams — to train as a psychotherapist and develop workshops
and seminars (and, ultimately, write this book).

2(c): Action

In previous chapters, we examined the power of taking small
steps forward to help us overcome resistance to change. Similarly,
in expressing our drive for meaning, we can implement this strategy by creating a plan of action and appreciating that every act
counts. The Talmud itself warns about the dangers of being overly
ambitious, as it says, "He who grabs too much, grabs nothing."[130]

The Rambam explains that we should look at the world as balanced — half meritorious and half lacking merits — and on the
verge of destruction, and that one positive action has the power
to make the difference.[131]

There is a beautiful story that illustrates the profound value of
simple actions that reflect our care for the world.

A man called Choni was walking on the road and
saw another man planting a carob tree. Choni asked
him, "How long will it take for this tree to bear fruit?"
The man replied, "Seventy years." Choni then asked
him, "And do you think you will live another seventy
years and eat the fruit of this tree?" The man answered,

"Perhaps not. However, when I was born into this world, I found many carob trees planted by my father and grandfather. Just as they planted trees for me, I am planting trees for my children and grandchildren so they will be able to eat the fruit of these trees."[132]

By filling our days with good deeds, we enrich our lives with a deeper sense of meaning. When Abraham was approaching the end of his life, he was described as "coming with his days" (as opposed to the "coming with the years of his life"), because each of his days was filled with good deeds.[133]

A story is told about a rabbi who died at the age of fifty. When the family returned from the funeral, the eldest son said, "Our father had a long life." Everyone was shocked, "How can you say that of a man who died so young?" they asked. "Because his life was full, he wrote many important books and touched many people," he replied.

Stage 3: Transformation

In our desire to live a deeply meaningful life, we often encounter traits and habits that hold us back, such as lack of confidence, laziness, and procrastination. In the Transformation stage, we look at going beyond merely overcoming the influence of these traits to stopping their influence completely by *transforming* them.

In Aaron's case, his fear of ridicule persisted even after he started helping victims of abuse. In his new work he was afraid of making mistakes and appearing inept. He started to train himself to gradually go beyond his fear of ridicule; he repeatedly took small steps forward to confront this fear. It took considerable time and effort, but this process slowly helped him to become more confident — until he had completely conquered his fear of ridicule.

We can use the same process of repeating positive acts to defeat any trait that is holding us back. When we succeed in our struggles and change our nature, we may also be able to use these experiences to help others with similar issues.

The psychiatrist Carl Jung wrote about this concept, which he called "the wounded healer."[134] The wounded healer is someone who has sought to heal his own wounds, and by so doing, has developed the compassion, wisdom, and strength to help others overcome theirs. He or she understands the pain of others, having also experienced it, and has become a gifted healer and a source of inspiration to those around them. We, too, become wounded healers by changing our character, and using our new capabilities to contribute more deeply to the lives of others.

Exercise

Awareness

1. Do you feel frustration that you are not using your abilities and talents in a more meaningful way?
2. Identify the causes and underlying traits which are holding you back.

Control

THOUGHT

3. What are the dreams, goals, or aspirations that you would love to achieve?
4. What is your life's purpose?

5. What would you give your life for?

6. Contemplate your mortality and ask yourself, "What do I want to achieve before I die"?

SPEECH

7. Discuss with a trusted person, friend, or therapist how you could express yourself more meaningfully and overcome what is holding you back.

ACTION

8. Create a plan to express yourself more meaningfully, breaking it down into manageable steps.

Transformation

9. Repeat positive actions that will help you uproot traits that hold you back from expressing yourself more meaningfully, and create a positive new habit.

Chapter 12

Spiritual Connection

God dwells wherever you let him in.

(The Kotzker Rebbe)

WE will now look at ways in which the development of a deeper spiritual connection with God, referred to in Hebrew as "*deveikus*," can help us to overcome psychological problems and bring greater fulfillment into our lives.

Jewish thought teaches that the deepest longing of the psyche is not for self-actualization, meaning, or to follow our instinctual drives. Rather, our deepest desire is for a spiritual connection, which is man's greatest pleasure and the goal of Judaism.[135]

> *This longing of the psyche for spirituality can be compared to a princess who marries a pauper. No matter how many gifts the pauper gives the princess, she will remain dissatisfied, as she is used to better things. So, too, the psyche is never fully satisfied with the pleasures of this world, but always longs for something higher — a spiritual connection.[136]*

Without this connection, man suffers from a deep lack of fulfillment and this can cause many psychological issues including addictions, anxiety, and depression. In the words of the philosopher Sartre, in referring to modern secular society,

"There is a God-shaped hole in the heart of man where the Divine used to be."[137]

There has been growing recognition in modern psychotherapy of the importance of the spiritual realm. Psychotherapy initially reflected an anti-religious slant, with Sigmund Freud viewing religion as a psychological crutch. The 1970s saw the development of the transpersonal school of psychotherapy, which teaches that healing and well-being are incomplete without the development of the spiritual dimension of life.

> "There is a God-shaped hole in the heart of man where the Divine used to be."

Roberto Assagioli, the founder of psychosynthesis, a transpersonal approach, explained that just as a person may be unaware of his instinctual drives, so too he may be unaware of his spiritual yearnings, which Assagioli called the "higher unconscious."[138]

Stage 1: Awareness

The first step in improving someone's psychological health through developing a deeper spiritual connection is to gain awareness of this longing and an understanding into the obstacles preventing its development.

Jewish thought teaches that we all have an intuitive appreciation of and connection to God, as the adage goes, "There are no atheists in a fox hole." There are many factors and misconceptions however, that can prevent us from appreciating this awareness and connection within ourselves.

> *A story is told of the Kotzker Rebbe, who once asked a student who had recently come to Kotzk (a small town in Poland) to learn with him.*
> *"Why have you come to study in Kotzk?"*
> *The student replied, "I have come here to find God."*

"It is unfortunate that you came so far and spent so much only to waste your time," the Rebbe countered. "God is everywhere. You could have found Him just as well had you stayed at home."

"If so, for what purpose should I have come?" the student asked.

"To find yourself," the Kotzker Rebbe answered.

Let's examine some common misconceptions that prevent people from developing their spirituality. We will start with philosophical issues.

- Science teaches all we can know is that which can be seen or measured with our senses. Religion is therefore viewed as anti-intellectual, antiquated, and contradictory to modern science.
- Early psychological teachings viewed a belief in God as a form of escape for people who were not strong enough to deal with life's problems.
- The problem of suffering, i.e., how does a caring God allow suffering?

Judaism is not based on blind faith; it is built on a rational understanding. There are logical explanations for the apparent contradictions between science and Judaism, as there are for how we can best understand suffering. (These issues are beyond the scope of this book and I have included suggested reading at the end of the book for those who wish to explore these topics further.)

On an emotional level, there are other factors that may come in to play. For example, often a person's relationship to God has been shaped by the understanding and experiences of their childhood and teenage years. If there were negative or uninspired experiences, a person may have little interest in — or even a repulsion to — spiritual development in later life.

> *A Catholic priest experienced an infestation of pigeons in his church. He contacted the local rabbi, whose synagogue was next door, to seek some advice. The rabbi explained to the priest that he had a method of getting rid of pigeons that never failed. He instructed the priest to gather all the pigeons together. Then the rabbi gave all the pigeons a bar mitzvah. "You won't have any more problems," the rabbi explained to the priest, "once I give someone a bar mitzvah, they never return!"*

Negative feelings may also arise through experiences with parents, teachers, peers, and authority figures. These emotions may then become transferred onto one's attitude to God. For example, if someone thinks authority figures are controlling and fear-inducing, he may project these feelings onto God; a person who felt abandoned by his or her parents may also feel angry and abandoned by God.

Rabbi Luzzatto explained that there are also those who will admit that spiritual development is important but they become distracted by other activities, causing their spiritual activities to become rote and meaningless.[139]

Stage 2: Control

If there are strong feelings of anger or trust issues affecting a relationship with God, I would suggest a person revisit the chapters on anger and self-esteem to best deal with them.

For many others, developing spirituality is not seen as important, beneficial, or pleasurable — some even view it as irrelevant. It is therefore important to understand the value of a relationship with God, and experience the benefits of a deeper spiritual connection.

In mystical sources, creation is described as occurring through a gradual concealment of the divine light until there reached a point where almost all of the light was concealed. God is thus "hidden" within the physical world.[140]

To separate from that which blocks our spirituality, we need to choose to overcome this concealment and connect to the Divine. As the Zohar explains, "an awakening from below creates an awakening above."[141] This means that when a person takes a step toward God, God moves closer to that person, and the person can feel increased spirituality in his life.

Let's explore how we can do this, with examples that use our faculties of thought, speech, and action.

2(a): Thought

One way to use the thought process to attain a deeper authentic spiritual connection is to reflect on the wonders of nature. Compare the physical world to a work of art. Just as a painter expresses himself in his paintings and one can recognize the artist's nature in his work, we too can perceive God in His handiwork, the physical world. As Albert Einstein said, "All the wondrous laws of nature testify to the existence of God who created the universe."[142]

The Rambam explained that when we contemplate nature and see its magnificence, we will be struck by a sense of awe and a longing for spiritual closeness.[143]

> "All the wondrous laws of nature testify to the existence of God who created the universe."

When my wife was pregnant with our first child, we went for an ultrasound early in the pregnancy and we saw the baby for the first time. When the doctor pointed out the baby's backbone on the scan, I was amazed. When I saw the heart beating, I was hit by a sense of awe: the heart pumps blood every second of a person's life.

A person can contemplate and study any aspect of nature — the human body, plant life, or animal life — and be struck by this sense of awe.

The human brain weighs three pounds and has about one hundred billion neurons (nerve cells), the same number of stars in our galaxy. During early pregnancy, the rate of neuron growth is 250,000 neurons a minute. Each neuron has 10,000 to 100,000 fibers that contact other neurons, making approximately 10 trillion connections.[144] All the telephone cables in the world comprise of a small fraction of this number,[145] and more electrical impulses are generated in one day by a single human brain than by all the telephones in the world.[146]

We can also connect with the transcendent pleasure of closeness to God by experiencing moments of breathtaking natural beauty, such as a beautiful sunset or a spectacular view of the stars at night.

Toward the end of his life, Rabbi Samson Raphael Hirsch, the spiritual leader of German Jewry in the nineteenth century, decided to travel to see the Alps. As he was old and unable to travel easily, his congregants asked him for an explanation. "When I get up to Heaven, I want to have an answer when God says to me, "Samson, did you visit my beautiful Alps?"[147]

> *When I was seventeen years old, I went on holiday to Amsterdam. One afternoon I decided to take a walk in a local park. It had just stopped raining, and the hues of the green foliage were very intense, rain drops were dripping from the leaves, the sun began to shine through the branches, and the scent of flowers filled the air. As I turned a corner, a young man was playing a beautiful tune on a flute ("A Whiter Shade of Pale," by Procul Harum), and a small child was dancing spontaneously and laughing along to the music. At that moment I experienced an overwhelming sense of beauty and ecstatic joy.*

The psychologist Abraham Maslow describes these moments of spiritual connection as "peak experiences." Maslow developed exercises to help people achieve these peak experiences.[148] One of those exercises, similar to the Rambam's approach, was for people to meditate on nature by gazing at a very small flower intensely, with their total attention.

2(b): Speech

Speech can be used in many ways to create a spiritual connection. For our purposes, we will focus on prayer. The empowering nature of prayer is central to Jewish thought, whether a person prays in a formal or informal way. By praying with deeper *kavanah* (concentration or intention) and sharing our troubles with God, we can experience a deeper connection to Him. This can play a vital role in helping overcome many psychological problems such as anxiety, depression, and addiction.

> *A recent scientific study interviewed 246 people before they underwent cardiac surgery. The results showed that those who prayed before the operation were less anxious and more optimistic regarding the outcome.[149]*

At the core of Alcoholics Anonymous and other twelve-step programs is the idea that we cannot succeed alone, but only by turning for help to "a higher power."[150] This understanding has played an important role in helping countless people to overcome despair, and in empowering them to transform their lives by praying to God.

> *Robert became a drug addict in his youth and at the age of sixteen was sent to rehab. It was a terrifying experience for him and he felt totally alone and at an all-time low. He was brought up in a religious Jewish family but had lost his faith. He described a*

transformational experience when, at a moment of utter despair, he fell to his feet and turned to God in prayer. This renewed connection helped him to defeat his addictions, and he went on to become a psychotherapist specializing in helping others to overcome drug addiction.

Turning to God for divine assistance is such a powerful step that the Talmud writes that if not for divine providence, we would be unable to defeat our self-deceptive side.[151]

2(c): Action

Jewish practice is filled with action-oriented practices. This is a vast and complex topic and many books have been written explaining their benefits. One example of using action to create an authentic connection to God is through observing the Shabbat, the day of rest.

Although on the surface it may appear to be a day of restrictions, in fact the opposite is true. Shabbat serves as an oasis in time; its message is to stop and take a break — *the world will not stop running without us.* It counters a tendency within us to get lost in work and to always strive for more. On Shabbat we spend time relaxing with family, praying, singing, learning, and enjoying the beauty of nature. We can reconnect with ourselves, our relationships, and strengthen our spiritual connection. The psychological benefits of a day of rest are many, and include building family closeness, reducing anxiety, and increasing gratitude. To paraphrase a section from the Shabbat morning prayers: "Were our mouths as full of song

"Were our mouths as full of song as the sea and our tongues as full of joy as its multitude of waves, our lips as full of thanks as the breadth of the heavens, we still could not thank you sufficiently."

as the sea and our tongues as full of joy as its multitude of waves, our lips as full of thanks as the breadth of the heavens, we still could not thank you sufficiently."[152]

Expressions of gratitude imbue life with a deeper sense of happiness, as happiness results from taking pleasure in the things that we have. The importance of developing a sense of gratitude in building emotional wellbeing has been demonstrated by scientific research.

> *In an experiment, psychologists Dr. Robert A. Emmons and Mike McCullough of the University of California asked participants to write a few sentences each week, focusing on particular topics. One group wrote about things they were grateful for that had occurred during the week. A second group wrote about daily irritations or things that had displeased them, and the third wrote about events that had affected them with no emphasis on whether these events were positive or negative. After ten weeks, those who had written about gratitude were more optimistic and felt better about their lives.[153]*

Stage 3: Transformation

In the Transformation stage, we reach beyond having a spiritual connection to forming a deeper sense of God's reality in our life. The psychiatrist Carl Jung called the journey of transformation a "journey to meet the self and simultaneously to meet the Divine."[154] When he was asked whether he believed in God, he replied, "I don't *believe* in God, I *know* there is a God."[155]

In Jewish thought this level is known as doing something with all your heart, "*b'chol levavcha*," which refers to the true self and the self-deceptive side working together without conflict. Like all the other transformational changes, it occurs as a result of positive repetition, in this case, the repetition of spiritual practices which change our nature.

In fact, all the transformations we have described in previous chapters, in which a person changes character traits, help us achieve this level of spiritual transformation. By changing our nature from being (for example) self-centered, greedy, or impatient to generous, patient, or assertive, we become more God-like. This, in turn, enables us to appreciate God's reality and goodness in a more profound way.

Often, there is one specific negative trait that is at the root of problems in our self, relationships, and spiritual life. When we transform that trait, we transform every aspect of our lives.

One of the beneficial aspects of building this deeper relationship with God is that we begin to recognize the situations in which we find ourselves, and the problems we experience, as purposeful. This realization can help us to build a greater sense of hope at times of despair and trust that good will result from our challenges.

> *When Joseph was sold by his brothers into slavery, and when he was thrown into prison by Potiphar, he could easily have despaired and fallen into a deep depression. But during those twenty-two years of separation from his family, the understanding that there was a divine purpose to his suffering gave him hope. Its purpose was revealed later, when he rose to become viceroy of Egypt and saved his family and Egypt from starvation.[156]*

The purpose of our challenges, as explained in Jewish thought, is to help us bring out the true self, our inner greatness, and form a closeness to God. The Hebrew word for test, or ordeal, is *nisayon* — from the root word *nes*, meaning "flag" — as through our tests, we show our true nature, our flag.[157]

The idea that challenges are purposeful and are for our own benefit is also found in psychotherapy, and is known as the "repetition compulsion."[158] The repetition compulsion is the subconscious tendency of a person to be drawn into situations that mirror past traumatic experiences in order that he might achieve a belated mastery of them. Thus, on both a spiritual and a psychological level, problems are vehicles for growth with the potential to bring hope and meaning into our lives.

With the tremendous psychological benefits spirituality brings (of which we have only mentioned a few), it is not surprising that Martin Seligman claims that spiritual engagement is one of the key ingredients in creating a happy life.[159]

Exercise

Awareness

1. Become aware of times of spirituality in your life by thinking about moments of pleasure in nature or other experiences that you have had.
2. What is holding you back from a deeper spiritual connection?

Control

THOUGHT

3. Spend fifteen minutes a week studying an aspect of the wonders of nature.

SPEECH

4. Share your struggles and frustrations with God.

ACTION

5. Spend five to ten minutes appreciating your blessings on Shabbat.

Transformation

6. Repeat a spiritual practice so that you start to feel God's reality in your life.
7. See your problems as a divine gift. (*Complete the box on the following page.*)

Challenge / Problem	How would overcoming this challenge help you grow and benefit your life?
1.	
2.	
3.	

Chapter 13

Fulfilling Our Destiny

I place before you life and death... choose life.

(Deuteronomy 30:19)

MY goal in writing this book was not to produce a work of academia but to help people improve the quality of their lives. The key is to listen to our frustrations and pain, rather than ignore them, and to see how they are pushing us to grow, bring out our greatness, and develop a deeper spiritual connection.

The ACTive method requires us to look within in order to understand ourselves, and then to control self-defeating behaviors and to ultimately transform them. This is easier said than done, as we all have a desire to remain within our comfort zones. We may even deny that we have the power to change our lives at all. But in fact the opposite is true, as Victor Frankl eloquently pointed out: "Everything can be taken from a man but one thing: the last of the human freedoms — to choose one's attitude in any given set of circumstances, to choose one's own way."[160]

Rabbi Dessler illustrates this point with an example from the festival of Chanukah, when the Jewish People faced oppression by

> "Everything can be taken from a man but one thing: the last of the human freedoms — to choose one's attitude in any given set of circumstances, to choose one's own way."

the powerful Greek Empire, and all appeared to be lost. He writes that when all seems lost, we can either descend into despair or harness the power that lies within each of us to throw ourselves into succeeding. At the point where we undertake to succeed, we can find within ourselves new wellsprings of strength and assistance from Above. We can discover, in the depths of our darkness, a powerful new light.[161]

This was the decision the Jewish People made which helped them to miraculously win their war against the mighty Greeks. What seemed to be an impossible challenge was surmounted. This power lies within all of us and we, too, can reach the realm of the miraculous when we undertake to face our challenges.

When Abraham undertook the test of leaving his homeland, he was led to "the land that I will show you"[162] — a place of blessing, and he became a blessing to those around him. We, too, in our own way, when we "go to ourselves" and take a step into the unknown, arrive at a place of blessing. We gain a sense of joy, love, and inner fulfillment, and become a blessing to those around us as we turn our sorrow into joy, and our darkness into light.

Cognitive Therapy Techniques

Downward Arrow Technique

A. State worry

....

(Why does this matter?)

B. ....

(Why does this matter?)

C. ....

(Why does this matter?)

D. ....

2a) Thought Diary

Situation	Negative Thoughts	Evidence Supporting Negative Thoughts	Evidence Against Negative Thoughts	Alternative Perspective

Situation	Negative Thoughts	Evidence Supporting Negative Thoughts	Evidence Against Negative Thoughts	Alternative Perspective

2b) Thought Diary

Focusing on dealing with hot thoughts

Situation	Negative Thoughts (underline the hot thought)	Evidence Supporting Negative Thoughts	Evidence Against Negative Thoughts	Alternate Perspective

Biographies of Rabbis and Jewish Leaders

In alphabetical order by last name or, where known as such, by first name, popular name, or acronym

Alter of Novardok (1847–1919): Rabbi Yosef Yosel Horwitz, a student of Rabbi Israel Salanter, he founded Novardok, the *mussar* yeshiva.

Rabbi Bachya (1250–1320): Author of the ethical work, *Duties of the Heart*, lived in Spain.

Chofetz Chaim (1839–1933): Rabbi Israel Meir Kagan, considered the greatest sage of his time, lived in Radin, Belarus.

Choni HaM'agel (1st century BCE): A sage known for his piety, lived in Israel.

Rabbi Eliyahu E. Dessler (1892–1954): A prominent teacher of *mussar*, Russian-born, moved to England and later Israel.

Hillel the Elder (110 BCE–10 CE): A renowned sage and leader who lived in Jerusalem at the time of King Herod, led a school of sages of the Mishnah, the "students of Hillel."

Kotzker Rebbe (1787–1859): Rabbi Menachem Mendel Morgenstern of Kotzk, a leader of the Chassidic movement.

Rabbi Aryeh Levin (1885–1969): A Polish-born rabbi who lived in Jerusalem and was renowned for his piety.

Malbim (1809–1879): Rabbi Meir Leibush, a famed commentator on *Tanach* and rabbinical leader of many communities including Bucharest, Romania.

Rabbi Meir Simcha of Dvinsk (1843–1926): A prominent leader of East European Jewry in the early twentieth century and the Rabbi of Dvinsk, Lithuania for forty years.

Rabbi Moses ibn Ezra (1055–1138): A Jewish philosopher and poet, born in Spain.

Rabbi Nachman of Breslov (1772–1810): Founder of the Breslov Chassidic dynasty and great Chassidic master, lived in Uman, Ukraine.

Rabbi Tzadok HaCohen Rabinowitz (1823–1900): A Chassidic leader and prolific writer.

Rambam (1135–1204): Rabbi Moshe ben Maimon, also known as Maimonides. A great philosopher and codifier of Jewish Law. He lived in Spain and Morocco, and then in Egypt from 1170 until his death.

Ramchal (1707–1746): Rabbi Moshe Chaim Luzzatto, a prolific author of ethical, philosophical, and mystical works including *Path of the Just*. Born in Italy, and later lived in Amsterdam and then Israel.

Rashi (1040–1105): Rabbi Shlomo Yitzhaki, the foremost commentator on the Torah and Talmud, from Troyes, France.

Rabbi Israel Salanter (1810–1883): Rabbi Israel Lipkin of Salant, founder of the Mussar Movement, which stressed ethics and character perfection.

School of Hillel: A school of 1st-century sages who were students of Hillel the Elder.

School of Shammai: A school of 1st-century sages who were students of Shammai; they were often opponents of the students of Hillel in matters of Jewish Law.

King Solomon (931–970 BCE): King of Israel after his father, King David, he built the First Temple. He was known for his great wisdom, and authored Proverbs, Ecclesiastes, and Song of Songs.

Rabbi Moses Aaron Stern (1926–1998): Born in America, but lived most of his life in Israel, where he served as director of Yeshivas Kaminetz.

Rabbi Noach Weinberg (1930–2009): Founder and dean of Yeshivas Aish HaTorah in Jerusalem and a founder of the Jewish outreach movement.

Rabbi Shlomo Wolbe (1914–2005): A leading teacher of *mussar* in the 20th century.

Rabbi Yehoshua ben Chaninah (1st and 2nd centuries CE): A leading rabbi and teacher following the destruction of the Second Temple.

Rabbi Yehuda HaNasi (135–217): Leader of the Jewish People and compiler of the Mishnah.

Rabbenu Yonah of Gerona (1180–1263): Author of the famous ethical work, *Gates of Repentance*, lived in Catalonia, Spain.

Reb Zusha (1717–1800): Rabbi Meshulam Zusha of Anipoli, a great Chassidic rabbi.

Appendix 3

Psychotherapy —
Approaches and Personalities

In alphabetical order by last name or name of approach

Alcoholics Anonymous
Alcoholics Anonymous is a twelve-step program started in 1935 to help people overcome their drinking addiction. At the core of its approach is the concept that humans are powerless to overcome their addictions without turning to a higher power for help. The twelve-step approach is now used to help overcome a wide range of addictions including narcotics, overeating, and pornography.

Alfred Adler
Alfred Adler (1870–1937) was a psychiatrist who founded Individual Psychology. He parted company with Freud, viewing humans as understood within their social context.

Roberto Assagioli
Roberto Assagioli (1888–1974) was an Italian psychiatrist and pioneer in the fields of transpersonal psychotherapy. He founded the psychological approach known as psychosynthesis.

Attachment Theory
Attachment theory was developed by Richard Bowlby and Mary Ainsworth in the late 1950s and 1960s. It teaches that a child's healthy development comes from a stable attachment to its

primary caregiver. A dysfunctional relationship is seen at the root of social and emotional problems.

Aaron Beck

Aaron Beck (born 1921) is an American psychiatrist and a professor emeritus in the Department of Psychiatry at the University of Pennsylvania. He is regarded as the father of cognitive therapy (see below), having developed it in the 1950s.

Behavioral Therapy

Behavioral therapy was developed in the 1950s and 1960s as a reaction against Freudian psychoanalysis, which was viewed as being unscientific. The behavioral approach does not seek to understand the subconscious mind but focuses on changing self-destructive behavior using action-based techniques such as systematic desensitization, gradual exposure to the feared object, assertiveness training, and relaxation techniques. It is based on the premise that just as unproductive behaviors can be learned, they can also be unlearned.

John Bowlby

John Bowlby (1907–1990), a British psychoanalyst, was a pioneer of Attachment Theory and notable for his interest in child development.

Cognitive Behavioral Therapy (CBT)

Cognitive behavioral therapy was formed by the merger of cognitive therapy and behavioral therapy. It seeks to change faulty thinking and to replace it with rational thinking by using both cognitive and behavioral techniques

Cognitive Therapy

Cognitive therapy was developed in the 1950s by Aaron Beck and is based on the principle that our thinking influences the way we feel and act. Its goal is to replace irrational thinking with rational thought. This is achieved through a psycho-educational approach where clients learn to challenge their faulty thoughts, assumptions, and beliefs and replace them with effective cognition.

Albert Ellis

Albert Ellis (1913–2007) was an American psychologist who founded a cognitive behavioral approach, called rational emotive behavioral therapy, in 1955.

Existential Therapy

The existential approach is a psychological methodology that is based on insights from philosophy. It is not defined by any specific techniques but views humans as seeking to express themselves in a meaningful and authentic way. It seeks to help people achieve this by an exploration of their inner world to gain insight that gives them a more balanced view of their choices.

Victor Frankl

Victor Frankl (1905–1997) was the originator of logotherapy, an existential approach to therapy. He taught that the human's primary drive is for meaning. Logotherapy helps clients resolve their psychological issues by helping them find a greater sense of meaning in their lives.

Sigmund Freud

Freud (1856–1939) was the founder of psychoanalysis. He lived and worked in Vienna, Austria, until he fled to England in 1938 to escape the Nazis. He died in the United Kingdom the following year.

Gestalt Therapy

Gestalt Therapy is a humanistic approach developed by psychoanalyst Frederick Perls in the 1940s. It uses a range of experimental techniques to achieve self-actualization, including visualization, fantasy, role playing, and attention to verbal and non-verbal cues.

John Gottman

John Gottman (born in 1942) is a professor emeritus of psychology at the University of Washington who has done ground-breaking scientific research into marital stability and relationships.

Humanistic Psychotherapy

Humanistic psychotherapy emerged in the 1950s as a reaction against psychoanalysis and behavioral therapy which were seen as being too pessimistic and deterministic. Humanistic psychology views people as being driven to fulfill their unique potential, known as the drive for "self-actualization." It seeks to help people overcome problems by getting in touch with, and expressing more fully, their drive for self-actualization.

Imago Relationship Therapy

Imago relationship therapy was developed by Harville Hendrix and Helen LaKelly Hunt in the 1980s. It teaches that marriage is a source of spiritual growth which helps each person to heal their childhood wounds. Clients are taught to communicate in an open and constructive way. In this safe environment, they learn to understand each other, the dynamics of their relationship, and how to meet the needs of one another.

Carl Jung

Carl Jung (1875–1961) was the founder of analytic psychology. He was originally a student of Freud but disagreed with Freud's emphasis on instinctual drives and thus developed a more spiritual approach, viewing humans as striving for spirituality, meaning, and self-actualization.

Abraham Maslow

Abraham Maslow (1908–1970) was an American humanistic psychologist. He emphasized man's drive for self-actualization to use his full potential. He devised a theory of human motivation, known as Maslow's Hierarchy of Needs, starting with physical needs and ending with the highest need, the drive for self-actualization.

Person-Centered Therapy

Person-centered therapy is a humanistic approach developed by Carl Rogers in the 1940s and 1950s. It emphasizes a person's drive for self-actualization, and stresses the importance of a good relationship between client and therapist as the key to self-actualization. It considers that experiencing empathy, congruence, and being valued by one's therapist helps a client regain his ability to self-actualize and discover his own capacity to resolve his problems.

Positive Psychology

Positive psychology is a branch of psychology that uses scientific understanding and effective intervention to help achieve a satisfactory life, rather than treating mental illness. The focus of positive psychology is on personal growth rather than on pathology.

Psychoanalytic Therapy

Originated by Sigmund Freud in the late nineteenth century, psychoanalysis views behavior as being primarily motivated by unconscious drives which are instinctual in nature — sexuality and aggression. Its goal is to help clients gain more awareness into these subconscious drives and thereby to create more rational control.

Psychoanalytic therapy is continually evolving. Many later psychoanalytic thinkers, although maintaining their focus on the unconscious, disagreed with Freud's focus on instinctual drives and emphasized the importance of interpersonal relationships.

Psychosynthesis

Psychosynthesis is a psychotherapeutic approach developed by Roberto Assagioli in the early twentieth century. It views man as having a spiritual self which has higher aspirations, and it uses a range of techniques including guided imagery, affirmations, and meditation.

Martin Seligman

Martin Seligman (b. 1942), an American psychologist, is a former president of the American Psychological Association and the pioneer of positive psychology.

Transpersonal Therapy

Transpersonal therapy developed from humanistic psychology and became a formal discipline in the 1970s. It addresses the spiritual nature of the psyche and views psychological healing as incomplete if it has not addressed the spiritual realm.

Donald Winnicott

Donald Winnicott (1896–1971) was an English pediatrician and psychoanalyst who taught that the relationship between child and mother is imperative. He believed the majority of psychological problems were a consequence of poor parenting.

Irvin Yalom

Irvin Yalom (b. 1931), an American existential psychiatrist, is professor emeritus of psychiatry at Stanford University and author of many books on existential psychotherapy.

Appendix 4

Further Readings

Apisdorf, Shimon. *Rosh Hashanah Yom Kippur Survival Kit* (Leviathan Press).

Arush, Rabbi Shalom. *The Garden of Emuna* (Chut Shel Chesed Institutions).

Cohen, Adi. *We Are Not Alone* (Maagaley Yosher).

Kaplan, Rabbi Aryeh. *If You Were God* (Lehmanns).

Kaplan, Rabbi Aryeh. *Jewish Meditation: A Practical Guide* (Schocken).

Kelemen, Lawrence. *Permission to Believe* (Targum Press).

Kelemen, Lawrence. *Permission to Receive* (Targum Press).

Kornbluth, Doron. *Jewish Matters* (Mosaica Press).

Pliskin, Rabbi Zelig. *Gateway to Happiness* (Jewish Learning Exchange).

Schroeder, Dr. Gerald. *Genesis and the Big Bang* (Bantam).

Schroeder, Dr. Gerald. *The Science of God*, (Free Press).

Spiro, Ken. *Crash Course in Jewish History* (Targum Press).

Weinberg, Rabbi Noach. *What the Angel Taught You* (Mesorah Publications Ltd).

Websites: www.aish.com

Glossary

Bar Mitzvah — When a Jewish boy turns thirteen and becomes accountable for religious observance. This word is often used for the synagogue ceremony that marks this time of his life.

Bilam — An evil prophet mentioned in the Torah. He tried to curse the Jewish People when they encamped in the wilderness after leaving Egypt.

Chanukah — An eight-day Jewish holiday commemorating the rededication of the Holy Temple (the Second Temple) in Jerusalem at the time of the Maccabean revolt against the ancient Greek Seleucid Empire of the second century BC.

Chassid/Chassidic — A person or group who follows Chassidism (see below).

Chassidism — A Jewish Orthodox movement founded by Rabbi Yisrael Baal Shem Tov in the early eighteenth century in Eastern Europe.

Chavruta — A learning partner.

Cheder — An elementary school or classes of Jewish studies.

Concise Code of Jewish Law — A contemporary compilation of basic laws of Jewish life that are germane today.

Ethics of the Fathers — The tractate of the Mishnah devoted to ethics and moral teachings.

Gemara — The Talmud.

HaNasi — The prince, or president, of the Jewish People.

Kabbalah — Jewish mystical teachings.

Korach — He led a rebellion against Moses' leadership when the Jews were traveling in the wilderness.

Neshamah — The highest level of the psyche, also used as a name for the entire soul.

Nefesh — The lowest level of the psyche, the life force.

Mishnah — The first compilation of the oral law, authored by Rabbi Yehudah HaNasi (approx. 200 CE).

Mussar — Torah ethical and moral teachings.

Mussar Movement — A movement among European Jewry in the early nineteenth century, started by Rabbi Salanter, with the aim of revitalizing the importance of self-improvement.

Purim — The Jewish holiday that commemorates the saving of the Jewish People in the ancient Persian Empire from Haman, who was planning to kill all the Jewish People.

Rabbeinu — Our teacher or rabbi.

Rebbe — A teacher or Chassidic rabbi/master.

Rosh HaYeshiva — The dean of an academy of Jewish learning.

Ruach — The middle level of the psyche.

Shabbos — The Sabbath.

Sitra achra — The irrational side of the psyche.

Synagogue — A communal place of prayer for people practicing Judaism.

Tanach — An acronym for the Pentateuch, Prophets, and Writings.

Talmud — Compendium of the Oral Law tradition in the lands of Israel and Babylon between 200–500 CE.

Teshuvah — Repentance.

Tisha B'Av — The fast day that commemorates the destruction of the first and second Temples. It falls on the ninth of the month of Av in the Jewish calendar.

Tochachah — Constructive criticism.

Torah — The Pentateuch, also used to describe the entire body of traditional Jewish literature.

Yom Kippur — The Day of Atonement.

Yeshiva — Institution of higher Jewish education or rabbinical college.

Zohar — The principal book of Jewish mysticism.

Zt"l — A Hebrew acronym, meaning "may the memory of a righteous one be a blessing."

Notes

Introduction

1   Genesis 12:1.

2   *Sfas Emes, Parshas Lech Lecha.*

3   Rabbi Yisrael Salanter, *Ohr Yisrael*, Letter 30.

Chapter 1

4   Talmud, *Niddah* 30b.

5   Proverbs, 20:5.

6   Talmud, *Sukkah* 52a.

7   Talmud, *Sukkah* 52a.

8   *Nefesh HaChaim*, Gate 2, ch. 16.

Chapter 2

9   Rabbi Dr. Z.F. Ury, *The Story of Rabbi Yisrael Salanter*, p. 43.

10 *Ohr Yisrael*, Letter 30.

11 *Ohr Yisrael*, Letter 30.

12 *Ohr Yisrael*, Letter 30.

13 *Etz Peri*, p.13, par. 5.

14 *Tevunah*, p.15.

15 Rabbi S. Wolbe, *Alei Shur*, Vol. 1, p. 159.

16 Rabbi Moshe C. Luzzatto, *Path of the Just*, ch. 3.

17 Genesis 3:12–13.

18 Rabbi Aryeh Kaplan, trans., *Stories of Rabbi Nachman*, p. 481.

19 *The Concise Book of Jewish Law* 1:4.

20 Talmud, *Tamid* 32a.

21 Rabbi Salanter, *Iggeres Hamussar.*

22 Proverbs 12:25.

23   Rabbi N. Wolpin, *Torah Personalities*, p. 113.

24   *Anaf Yosef* on *Yoma* 75a.

25   *Sefer HaChinuch*, Mitzvah 16.

26   D. Sofer, *Rav Yosef Yoizel Horowitz, zt"l, The Alter of Novardok.*

27   Rabbi Aryeh Kaplan, trans., *Stories of Rabbi Nachman*, p. 479.

28   Rambam on *Pirkei Avos* 3:18.

29   Zohar 1:4a.

30   Talmud, *Eruvin* 53b.

31   Proverbs 22:3.

Chapter 3

32   B. Cortright, *Psychotherapy and the Spirit.*

33   G. Corey, *Theory and Practice of Counseling and Psychotherapy*, 5th Ed., 95–96.

34   D. Burns, *The Feeling Good Handbook*, p. 8.

35   C. Rogers, *On Becoming a Person.*

36   V. Frankl, *The Will to Meaning*, p. 105.

37   G. Corey, *Theory and Practice of Counseling and Psychotherapy*, 5th Ed., p. 317.

Chapter 4

38   D. Burns, *Feeling Good*, 263–270.

39   Numbers, ch. 13–14.

40   Proverbs 12:25.

41   Talmud, *Yoma* 75a.

42   Rashi on Genesis 32:10.

43   D. Burns, *The Feeling Good Handbook*, p. 242.

44   *Chovos HaLevovos*, Gate 4.

Chapter 5

45   M. Seligman. In J. Buie, "'Me' Decades Generate Depression: Individualism Erodes Commitment to Others," *APA Monitor* 19 (October 1988):18.

46 Westbrook, Kennerley and Kirk, *An Introduction to Cognitive Behaviour Therapy*, p. 165.

47 G. Butler and T. Hope, *Manage Your Mind*, p. 257.

48 Ethics of the Fathers 6:6.

49 Heard from Rabbi Noach Weinberg, *zt"l.*

50 Talmud, *Kesubos* 59a.

51 https://en.wikipedia.org/.../ If_You're_Going_Through_Hell

52 "Effects of Exercise Training on Older Patients with Major Depression," *Arch Intern Med.* 1999;159(19): 2349–2356.

53 G. Butler and T. Hope, *Manage your Mind*, p. 269.

Chapter 6

54 Talmud, *Sanhedrin* 37a.

55 Rabbi Daniel Yaakov Travis, heard from a student of the Chazon Ish.

56 Numbers 13:33.

57 Heard from Rabbi Noach Orlowek.

58 Dr. E. Bowlby, *Attachment*, Vol. 1 (1967).

59 Nancy DuVergne Smith, "How Schools Shortchange Girls" <http://members.aol.com/nancyds/girls.html

60 *Rabbeinu Yonah al HaTorah*, p. 156.

61 H.L. Ansbacher and R.R. Ansbacher, ed., *The Individual Psychology of Alfred Adler — A Systematic Presentation in Selections from His Writings* (New York: Basic Books Inc., 1956) p. 259.

62 M. Seligman, *Authentic Happiness*, p. 135.

63 M. Seligman, *Authentic Happiness*, p. 28.

64 *Alei Shor*, Vol. II, 158–160.

65 Genesis, ch. 49.

66 Leviticus 19:18.

Chapter 7

67 www.hsph.harvard.edu › News › In the News
68 Book of Esther 5:9.
69 Talmud, *Eruvin* 65a.
70 Ethics of the Fathers 2:5.
71 Ethics of the Fathers 1:6.
72 Leviticus 19:18.
73 *Chovos HaTalmidim*, ch. 19.
74 www.lettersneversent.com/pages/about
75 Talmud 31a.

Chapter 8

76 Genesis 4:3–6.
77 *Kli Yakar*, Genesis 4:1.
78 *Michtav M'Eliyahu*, Vol. 3, p. 302.
79 *Shem Mishmuel, Parshas Balak*.
80 Wings, *Wings over America*.
81 Ethics of the Fathers 4:1.
82 Talmud, *Bava Basra* 21a.
83 *Ksav Sofer* on Genesis 4:15.
84 Exodus 14:4.

Chapter 9

85 Wikipedia.org/wiki/Divorce_demography
86 M.D.S. Ainsworth, M. C. Blehar, E. Waters, and S. Wall, *Patterns of Attachment: A Psychological Study of the Strange Situation* (Hillsdale, NJ: Earlbaum, 1978).
87 Talmud, *Kiddushin* 70b.
88 E. Fromm, *The Art of Loving*, p. 94.
89 H. Hendrix, *Getting the Love You Want*, p. 75.
90 Proverbs 18:21.
91 J. Gottman and N. Silver, *The Seven Principles of Making Marriage Work*, p. 40.
92 *Alei Shur* 2, Gate 4, section 4.

93   Talmud, *Eruvin* 13b.

94   H. Hendrix, *Getting The Love You Want*, p. 143.

95   C. Rogers, *On Becoming a Person*, p. 207.

96   H. Hendrix, *Keeping the Love You Find*, p. 284.

97   Poem by Rabbi Moses Ibn Ezra.

98   *Michtav M'Eliyahu*, Vol. 1.

99   Talmud, *Bava Metzia* 32b.

100 Proverbs 27:19.

101 Talmud, *Sotah* 17a.

102 R. Kosta Mikveh Yisrael.

103 Genesis 2:24.

104 *A Tzaddik in Our Time*, p. 150.

105 Wikipedia, https://en.wikipedia.org/wiki/
Milgram_experiment

Chapter 10

106 Wikipedia https://en.wikipedia.org/wiki/
Chiune_Sugihara

107 Mishnah Torah, Book of Knowledge 2:2.

108 Rashi on Genesis 4:9.

109 Talmud, *Yoma* 87a.

110 Mishnah Torah, Book of Knowledge, Laws of Teshuvah 2:1.

111 Ethics of the Fathers 2:1.

112 D. Burns, *The Feeling Good Handbook*, p. 113.

113 Talmud, *Avodah Zarah* 17a.

Chapter 11

114 Talmud, *Sanhedrin* 38a.

115 *Kaddish*, ArtScroll Mesorah Series, p. xxiv.

116 V. Frankl, *Man's Search for Meaning*, p. 126.

117 V. Frankl, *Man's Search for Meaning*, p. 129.

118 C.G. Jung, *Modern Man in Search of a Soul* (New York &
London, Harvest Books, 1933), p. 229.

119 Rabbi Moshe C. Luzzatto, *Path of the Just*, ch. 3.

120 V. Frankl, *The Unheard Cry for Meaning*, p. 19.

121 V. Frankl, Man's Search for Meaning, p. 130.

122 Proverbs 26:13.

123 Rabbi Moshe C. Luzzatto, *Path of the Just*, ch. 3.

124 Heard from Rabbi N. Weinberg, *zt"l.*

125 Ecclesiastes 7:2.

126 I. Yalom, *Staring at the Sun*, p. 33.

127 *Chofetz Chayim al HaTorah, Parshas Chukas.*

128 Wikipedia.org/wiki/Alfred_Nobel

129 K. Douglas, *Climbing the Mountain.*

130 Talmud, *Sukkah* 5a.

131 Mishnah Torah, *Sefer Mada*, Laws of Teshuvah 3:4.

132 Talmud, *Taanis* 23a.

133 *Likkutei Sichot*, Vol. XXXV, p. 91.

134 C.G. Jung, *Psychology of the Unconscious*, p. 181.

135 Rabbi Moshe C. Luzzatto, *Path of the Just*, ch. 1.

Chapter 12

136 Rabbi Moshe C. Luzzatto, *Path of the Just*, ch.1.

137 K. Amstrong, *The Battle for God*, p. 119.

138 R. Assagioli, *Psychosynthesis*, p. 17.

139 Rabbi Moshe C. Luzzatto, *Path of the Just*, Introduction.

140 Rabbi Aryeh Kaplan, *Inner Space*, ch. 2.

141 Zohar 1.

142 H. Gutsteiner, psychology lecturer from an interview with Albert Einstein in Beliefs by Y. Has, University of Bar Ilan.

143 Mishnah Torah, Book of Knowledge, Fundamental of Torah 2:2.

144 https://faculty.washington.edu/chudler/facts.html

145 A. Katz, T. Cohen, *Our Amazing World: Wonders Hidden Below the Surface.*

146 S. Juan, *The Odd Brain: Mysteries of Our Weird and Wonderful Brains.*

147 www.jewishpathways.com/files/Travel

148 A. H. Maslow, *Toward a Psychology of Being.*

149 Gerontologist 42(1), p. 70–81.

150 Bill W., *Alcoholics Anonymous*, ch. 5.

151 Talmud, *Kiddushin* 30b.

152 The ArtScroll Siddur, Wasserman Edition, p. 400.

153 Emmons RA, et al. "Counting Blessings Versus Burdens: An Experimental Investigation of Gratitude and Subjective Well-Being in Daily Life," *Journal of Personality and Social Psychology* (Feb. 2003): Vol. 84, No. 2, 377–89.

154 Crowley, Vivianne, *Jung: A Journey of Transformation: Exploring His Life and Experiencing His Ideas* (Wheaton Illinois: Quest Books, 2000).

155 M.S. Peck, *Further Along the Road Less Travelled*, p. 174.

156 Genesis 45:5.

157 M. Seligman, *Authentic Happiness*, p. 260.

Chapter 13

158 Donald C. Abel, *Freud on Instinct and Morality*, p. 43.

159 *Bereishis Rabbah* 55:1.

160 V. Frankl, *Man's Search for Meaning*, p. 86.

161 Rabbi E. Dessler, *Sanctuaries in Time*, p. 154.

162 Genesis 12:1.

About the Author

Aryeh Sampson holds a master's degree in psychotherapy and counseling and is an accredited member of the British Association of Counseling and Psychotherapy. He has received rabbinical ordination and earned a master's degree in Jewish studies.

Aryeh has a private practice in individual and couples counseling in North London and counsels internationally by phone and Skype. He also gives workshops and seminars on psychotherapy and Judaism. He lives with his wife and children in London, England.

For more information about counseling or workshops or to receive the *Go to Yourself* newsletter, visit www.aryehsampson.com or email info@aryehsampson.com.

About Mosaica Press

Mosaica Press is an independent publisher of Jewish books. Our authors include some of the most profound, interesting, and entertaining thinkers and writers in the Jewish community today. Our books are available around the world. Please visit us at www.mosaicapress.com or contact us at info@mosaicapress.com. We will be glad to hear from you.